THE COMPLETE GUIDE TO
CARING FOR YOUR

HORSE

THE COMPLETE GUIDE TO
CARING FOR YOUR
HORSE

Bernadette Faurie
and
Penny Swift

NEW
HOLLAND

Above: *Supple leather and gleaming metal are the signs of well-maintained tack.*

Half title: *To a domesticated horse, the freedom of the open plains may be part of a distant collective memory, but it is never quite forgotten.*

Full title: *Horses can be highly rewarding animals that bring their owners much joy.*

First published in 2004 by New Holland Publishers Ltd
London • Cape Town • Sydney • Auckland
www.newhollandpublishers.com

Garfield House	80 McKenzie Street	14 Aquatic Drive	218 Lake Road
86 Edgware Road	Cape Town	Frenchs Forest	Northcote
London W2 2EA	8001	NSW 2086	Auckland
United Kingdom	South Africa	Australia	New Zealand

Copyright © 2004 New Holland Publishers (UK) Ltd

Copyright © 2004 in text: Bernadette Faurie and Penny Swift

Copyright © 2004 in illustrations: New Holland Publishers (UK) Ltd

Copyright © 2004 in photographs: Struik Image Library (SIL) and
New Holland Image Library (NHIL/Janek Szymanowski) and individual
photographers and/or their agents listed on page 192.

Publisher: Mariëlle Renssen
Publishing managers: Claudia dos Santos, Simon Pooley
Senior designer: Geraldine Cupido
Editor: Leizel Brown
Designer: Janine Clocte
Illustrations: Steven Felmore and Anton Krügel
Production: Myrna Collins
Consultant: Mary Kay Kinnish

ISBN 1 84330 592 5

Reproduction by Hirt & Carter Cape (Pty) Ltd
Printed and bound in Singapore by Kyodo Printing Co

CONTENTS

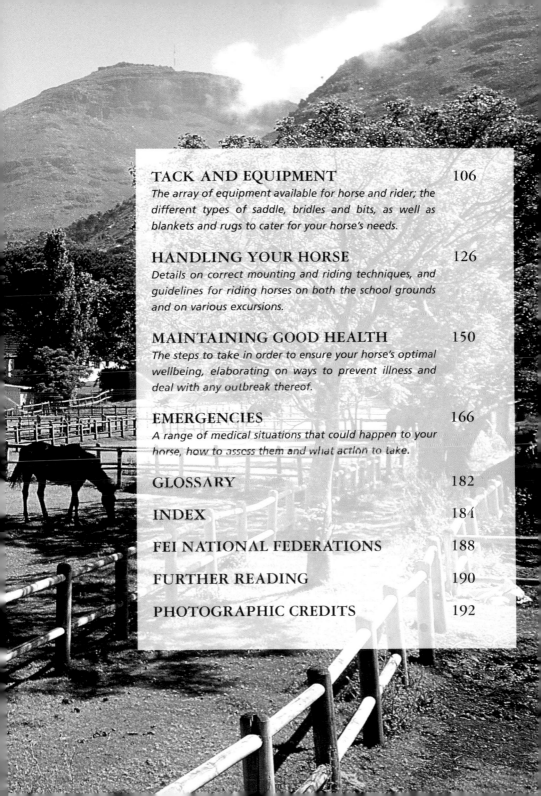

HISTORY AND DEVELOPMENT

The evolution of the horse is one of the best documented of all mammals due to an exceptionally complete fossil record, which suggests that the forerunners of the modern horse were forest browsers on the American continent.

Fifty million years ago, the prototype of the horse was only about the size of a fox. Unlike today's horse, it had toes instead of hooves (three on the back feet and four on the front), and its skull and teeth were suitably adapted for browsing on leaves in the swampy forests and woodlands of its prehistoric home.

This was *Hyraco-therium*, also called *Eohippus*, or 'dawn horse' (from the Greek *eos* – dawn) the forerunner of the present-day horse.

Over millions of years, as the climate and vegetation gradually changed, *Eohippus* evolved into *Mesohippus*, a sheep-sized, browsing animal with longer legs and neck, and, again, toes instead of hooves. Between 25 and 10 million years ago, *Merychippus* appeared. Pony-sized, but still retaining a three-toed foot, *Merychippus* marked the transition from a browsing to a grazing animal. It lived on the great plains and grasslands that proliferated across what is now

northern Europe and America, at a time when the ice caps melted and the forests thinned.

By the time of *Pliohippus* (about 7 to 2.5 million years ago), we see the development of the single toe (hoof), an increase in all-round strength and speed and more horselike features. The final stage in the evolutionary chain was *Equus*, which appeared less than two million years ago, and is the forerunner of today's modern horses and other related species, such as asses and zebras.

During the Pleistocene era, which lasted from 2.5 million to 10,000 years ago, *Equus* slowly migrated from the forests and plains of the Americas to the open Eurasian steppes via the land bridge that emerged across what is now the Bering Strait, between Asia and America. Between 10,000 and 8000 years ago, the horse vanished from both North and South America, not to appear again on its native continent until it was reintroduced by the Spanish explorers and conquistadors of the 16th century.

Despite its disappearance in the Americas, *Equus* continued to flourish in the 'old world', with the modern horse, *Equus caballus,* becoming widespread throughout central Asia and Europe.

Left: *Alert and watchful, these Lipizzaner mares embody the beauty and grace of horses.*
Inset: *Horses are represented in cave art, such as that found in Lascaux, France, which dates from c15,000BC.*

By the Mesolithic era, from about 12,000–3,000BC, the ice sheets were once again retreating northward. In southern Europe, this was followed by the Neolithic period (9000–2400BC), which marks the transition from the nomadic life of the hunter-gatherer to the beginnings of settlement, cultivation and the domestication of animals. Horses were probably first domesticated during the Neolithic era by the tribes that inhabited the steppes around the Black and Caspian seas. Although the first domesticated horses were used most likely as draught animals, pulling wagons with solid wheels, it could not have been long before man realized the advantages of riding and began to breed horses for his own use.

The development of civilization is linked to man's relationship with the horse. Being mounted gave early man a different perspective on his world and a new understanding of his role in shaping the environment around him. He was able to cover greater distances in search of food, and the ability to get closer to his prey was a significant survival factor in those harsh times. As a means of transport and conveyance, horses enabled man to expand his boundaries, bringing him into contact, and often conflict, with other tribes and clans. From the earliest times, the horse has played a vital role in war and conquest, exploration and colonization.

As early man migrated southward, seeking ever warmer climates, he settled in the Fertile Crescent valley formed by the Tigris and Euphrates rivers of ancient Mesopotamia (modern-day Iran and Iraq). This pastoral way of life was disrupted by the great floods of c3000BC, which swept away many of the ancient civilizations and paved the way for the great cultures upon which modern history is based.

Records dating from the Middle Kingdom of Egypt (c2000–1500BC) document the use of horse-drawn chariots by the Hyksos, or Shepherd Kings, who dominated upper Egypt and the delta area. Horse-drawn chariots were also used in the conquest of Phoenicia and Palestine during the New Kingdom (1570–715BC). Horses were used for hunting, riding and warfare during the powerful Mycenaean empire of Crete (c1900–1200BC), and probably brought to Greece between 800–700BC by the Scythians, who were instrumental in developing the art of horsemanship and riding for pleasure.

The origins of the tack and equipment we use today are rooted equally far back in time. The use of saddles, stirrups and nailed-on shoes can be traced to the Chinese in pre-Christian times. Evidence of the first bits, dating to 1500BC, suggest they were used by the nomadic tribes of the Ukraine, although the earliest examples were probably used for driving rather than riding. Even much later, when the Arabs started to ride, they used a type of adapted bitless halter, the *haqma*, a term which became anglicized into the present word for a bitless bridle, the hackamore.

It was in Greece that the horse first began to appear more frequently as a subject in literature, art, pottery and relief sculpture, such as the friezes on the Parthenon in Athens. The Greek lyrical poet Sappho (c610–580BC) wrote 'On the black earth, say some, the thing most lovely is a host of horsemen ...' Around 400BC, Athenian soldier, historian and horseman, Xenophon, wrote a treatise entitled *Peri hippikes* (On the Art of Horsemanship).

Inset: *Equine art dating from the earliest times has been found throughout Europe and the Middle East.*

Xenophon's feeling for the horse is apparent throughout his work and many of his principles, particularly training by kindness rather than force, hold true to this day.

It is the stuff of legend that Alexander the Great (336–323BC) rode at the head of his conquering armies on Bucephalus, a horse no-one but the young Alexander was able to break. Having carried his master through the successful Asian campaigns, the horse died three years before Alexander and was buried on the banks of the Jhelum River in India.

Through war and peace, invasions and migrations, the horse propelled man on his journey through history, but the development of riding as an art was frozen with the demise of the Greek empire. The horse facilitated the expansion of the Roman empire from Hannibal to Hadrian; enabled mounted tribes from the eastern steppes, such as the Vandals, Franks and Goths, to invade central Europe in the 4th and 5th centuries; and took the Crusaders from Europe into the Holy Land, where they came into contact with skilled Arab horsemen and their desert-bred mounts.

It was the discovery of these fleet-footed Arabian horses, with their legendary stamina, intelligence and character, that was to have a profound influence on the later development of the horse.

The dominant image of the Middle Ages is of chain-mail-clad knights on large, heavily armoured horses. Jousting for their lady's favour in the pageantry of the tournament demanded gallantry of the knights rather than speed or manoeuvrability in their horses. However, on the battleground, the sheer weight of the knights' armour and weaponry, often as much as 400kg (900 lb), made fighting from horseback cumbersome and inefficient. This eventually gave rise to one of England's great tactical victories when, in 1415, Henry V's lightly equipped and highly mobile archers and foot soldiers defeated the heavily armoured French cavalry on the soggy ground of Agincourt. Ultimately, the discovery of gunpowder and the development of firearms in the 15th century made it possible for mounted warriors to discard some of their heavy armour. Speed, mobility and manoeuvrability were paramount for the type of warfare that guns delivered.

It was largely the possession of firearms and horses that enabled the Spanish conquistadors Hernán Cortés to defeat the Aztecs in Mexico, and Francisco Pizarro to overthrow the Inca kingdom in Peru, thereby reintroducing the horse to its original birthplace, the Americas.

Meanwhile, in Renaissance Europe, the ancient methods of training and riding horses were being rediscovered and explored, as riding academies allied to the royal courts were founded to provide equestrian education to young noblemen.

One of the pathfinders in this discovery was Frederico Grisone. His *Gli Ordini di Cavalcare* (The Orders of Riding) was published in 1552. Similar in many respects to the teachings of Xenophon, Grisone's methods lacked one significant aspect, that of harmony and understanding with the horse. It was a pupil of the Naples school, Frenchman Antoine de Pluvinel (1601–1643), a teacher of Louis XIII and author of *Manège Royal*, who promoted the enhancement of the horse's natural movements through training rather than the often brutal subjugation used by many during these times.

In 1733 François Robichon de la Guérinière published the first edition of his work *École de Cavalerie* (School of Cavalry), the fundamentals of which still form the basis, if not the 'bible', of the training system of the Spanish Riding School of Vienna, founded in the late 16th century and still regarded as the protectorate of classical riding.

Guérinière's greatest achievements include the development of the *selle à la français* (French saddle), still in use at the French cavalry centre, Cadre Noir, at Saumur, which enabled the development of the modern seat and leg position, as well as his composition of the first real riding instructions. As riding styles evolved, new horse breeds were developed for specific functions, such as hunting and carriage driving. For centuries, horses provided the chief means of transport; from the smallest Shetland pony working on island crofts to teams of matched pairs drawing elegant coaches through the cities and countryside of Europe, they were a central factor in the daily lives of many of the world's peoples.

Through war and peace, exploration and exploitation, the horse's influence on man's development remained unparalleled until the advent of the steam engine in 1769. The dawning of the Industrial Revolution changed the nature of man's dependence on the horse.

▶ UNDERSTANDING A HORSE'S SENSES ◀

To gain insight into how and why a horse reacts to things and situations, it is helpful to understand what the horse hears, sees and feels from its own perspective.

SIGHT

One often hears remarks on a particular horse's beautiful or expressive eyes. Horses have the largest eyes of any land mammal, and their eyes convey states of mind such as trust, uncertainty or fear. In common with most animals that are preyed upon, the horse's eyes are positioned on each side of its head, not at the front, affording it a very wide field of vision. With a huge field of peripheral vision available, the horse has only two blind spots, one directly behind it and the other around six feet directly in front of or beneath its nose, where vision is out of focus, at the least. If you walk

Above: *Positioned on each side of the head, the horse's eyes give it a wide field of vision.*

NORMAL EYE

WALLEYE

towards a horse, there comes a point where it can't focus on you, so it will turn its head away or back up until it can see you again. For example, when going to catch a horse from the field, the reaction described above could be interpreted as the horse not wanting to be caught when, in fact, if you approach from the side and the horse can keep you in sight, it will stand happily for you to reach it. If you stand behind a horse it will generally turn its whole body or head and neck to get a constant view, but a young or nervous horse can easily react with a warning kick to an intrusion it can't see.

Because of the position of its eyes, the horse needs to use its head and neck when reacting to visual stimuli. With the head held high, a horse can't see the ground in front of it. If you watch a horse pick its way across rough ground, you will notice that it will lower its head almost to the surface it is traversing. A strange or unfamiliar object on the ground or in a hedge

to its side, for example, will have the horse tilting its head to the side for a closer examination. If it is 'alien', the horse will pass the object with this sideways tilt of the head and a sideways step of the body. This forms the basis of shying, and in training it is important that the rider understands this impulse and gives the young horse a chance to look at the object. If the reaction is punished, either by design or by mistake when the rider becomes unbalanced and pulls on the reins, the horse rapidly learns to avoid such hazards in the future, which can be the foundation of a very real problem.

It was once thought that horses were colour blind, but evidence suggests the opposite – although horses seem to recognize yellows, greens and blues more easily than reds, purples and shades of grey.

Horses also have excellent long-range vision (picture a horse in the field gazing at something the human eye can't see) and good night vision.

Top left and right: *Eyes are usually brown. A walleye (also called a glass eye) is white or blue-white in colour due to a lack of pigment, but this does not affect the horse's eyesight.*

TOUCH

Horses are highly sensitive to touch. A horse can even feel a fly on its back (watch it twitch until it goes away), which is indicative of this acute sensitivity. When

being ridden, a horse that is unwilling to go forward despite the pressure exerted by the rider's leg will, nine times out of ten, have become desensitized by the misuse or overuse of the rider's leg signal. At all times, when riding or handling horses, a gentle but firm touch will yield the best results. The daily ritual of grooming helps to establish a positive sense of touch and is a soothing experience for the horse. This can be observed when a group of horses are together in the field, as mutual grooming is part of bonding and friendship among the herd.

Above: *Mutual grooming is a pleasurable pastime.*

HEARING

A horse's ears are very expressive. Apart from providing sensitive hearing, they are highly mobile, swivelling in the direction of the sound or stimulus that has drawn their attention. A dressage horse that is concentrating on its work will have its ears swivelled back softly in the direction of its rider, signalling that its attention is focused on the rider.

A horse attuned to some distant sound on the horizon will have its ears pointed forwards in the direction of the sound. An angry or upset horse can lay its ears flat

back, as if to block out the offending situation or noise.

Right: *The configuration of a horse's ears can indicate a range of emotions.*

SMELL

A horse's sense of smell is an important part of its behavioural pattern. Mares identify their foals by smell, as a stallion does an in-season mare.

Wild horses will find water by smell from some distance away and mountain ponies instinctively know how to use their sense of smell to avoid hazards.

Above: *When a horse assesses unusual smells, it is known as flehmen.*

TASTE

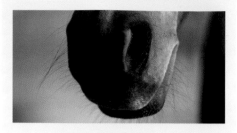

Horses generally like sweet-tasting food. Their natural senses of smell and taste will lead them to turn away from poisonous plants, which are generally bitter. A horse will quickly spit out an alien taste in the manger or after discovering a plant it doesn't like in a mouthful of sweet grass or hay. It can also easily develop a taste for treats, and soon learns to search pockets for carrots or sugar cubes.

Above: *Horses have well developed senses of smell and taste.*

VOCALIZATION

The sounds made by horses convey expressions, from the soft nicker of a mare to her foal and the shrill call of a stallion defending his territory to the whinny that greets the rider when he or she comes into the stable. In a horse being ridden, snorting or sneezing is mostly an expression of willingness, concentration and response to a command.

Right: *Whinnying is a means of communicating with stable mates.*

▶ IDENTIFICATION AND MARKINGS ◀

A universal identification system, or code of terminology, exists for describing the horse's colour, although it does tend to confuse those new to the horse world (for instance, why is a brown horse sometimes called a bay?). Breeding papers, passports and vaccination certificates all record in detail the horse's colour and markings so, theoretically, there should be no problem with matching papers to horse. When purchasing a horse, it is important to obtain these papers, as they provide the only means of identifying a particular animal.

A full description of a horse on its pedigree, passport or other documentation will contain details of its name, parentage, sex, breed or type, age, height, colour, markings on head, body and limbs, any distinguishing marks and acquired marks such as scars or brands.

Above: *Horses come in many colours. Seen here are (from left) black, roan, chestnut, brown, grey and bay.*

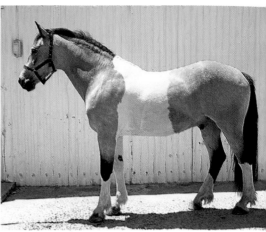
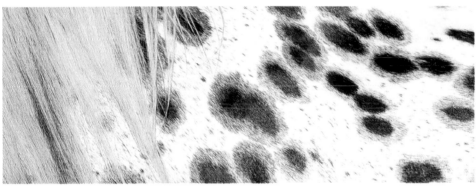

Above: *Appaloosa coat with marble pattern.*

Centre: *Appaloosa coat with leopard spots.*

Top Left: *Palomino – golden-cream with a flaxen mane and tail.*

Top Right: *Skewbald – patches of dun, white and brown.*

Colour classification largely depends on colour density, as not all horses have a coat of only one hair colour. Colours are defined as follows:

Black (1): The horse's coat, mane and tail must be black. No hairs of any other colour are allowed except for white markings.

Brown (2): The coat contains a mixture of black and brown hairs, forming generally a dark brown overall colour. The mane, tail and often the lower limbs will be of predominantly black hairs.

Bay (3): Body hair varies from mahogany to light brown in colour with black mane, tail and lower limbs.

In lighter bay horses, the coat around the flanks is almost toffee-coloured. A dark bay often has a lighter muzzle with black mane, tail and lower limbs.

Chestnut (4): Shades range from lightish brown (liver chestnut) to gold. The mane, tail and legs are the same colour as the coat or a shade darker, with no black hairs. The Palomino is a chestnut horse with a golden shine to the coat and a mane and tail of flaxen colour, but ideally as white as possible.

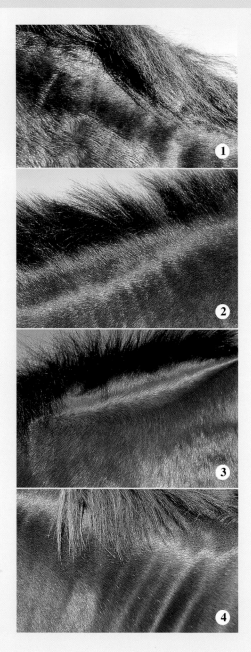

Roan (5): Any of the above colours, mixed with grey. Chestnut and grey combined is called strawberry roan; bay and grey result in a red roan; while a blue or grey roan has a mixture of black and grey hair.

Dun (6): The dun is a form of bay, with black points and generally a black stripe, known as an 'eel stripe', running the length of the back. To be termed dun, the coat colour would be yellowish- to mousey-grey.

Grey (7): As they age, grey horses generally lighten in colour to almost white or cream. A dappled grey has a mottled grey coat with darker patches.

Cream or Albino (8): White or cream hair on pink or unpigmented skin, often with pink or blue eyes.

Spotted horses (9): Also called coloured or pinto horses, these have a variegated coat, combining white with another colour in an irregular patchwork. They include the piebald, which has distinctive large patches of black and white; and the skewbald, which combines white with any colour other than solely black; and the spotted horse, such as the American-bred Appaloosa, which is characterized by spotted markings of different sizes and all colours. The coat patterns are known as blanket, marble, leopard, snowflake and frost.

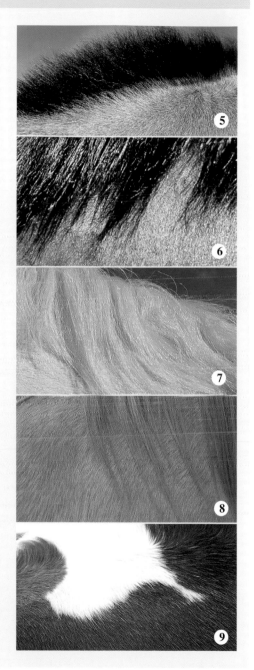

For the purpose of identification documents, descriptions of head and leg markings are very detailed and follow an internationally accepted format. For example, a blaze may be defined as: 'Wide blaze, irregular at top, extending to left at base'. There are a number of generally used terms that make it easy to identify any horse anywhere in the world. Other distinguishing coat marks are the eel stripe, a dark line extending down the back; the flesh mark, which is a patch of uncoloured skin; and the whorl, an often circular-shaped patch of hair that lies against the normal line of the coat.

BLAZE

STRIPE

STAR

SNIP

SOCKS

LONG SOCKS

STOCKING

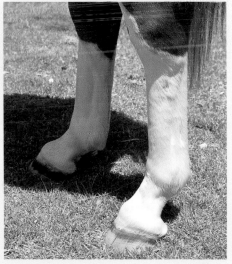

BRAND MARKS

These clearly defined symbols show the breeding district, or country of origin, of horses where such an identification system is used. In Germany, for example, horses are branded on the left thigh to show the breeding district they come from (such as Hanoverian, Westphalian, Bavarian). Mares registered to a studbook will also be branded with a registration brand on the left-hand side of the neck. Denmark, Sweden, Holland and other countries employ their own unique branding systems.

Although Thoroughbreds are not branded, they often have an identification number tattooed on the inside top lip, and those that are registered to Weatherbys, the international studbook control organization, usually have passports from birth.

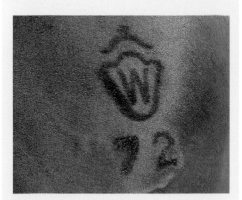

Above: *The brand mark of a Westphalian horse.*
Right: *The Arabian's dished face is a distinctive characteristic of the breed.*

Conformation is the term applied to the shape of the individual horse, how it is 'put together'. No horse is perfect, and horses with what may be termed less-than-perfect conformation should not be written off. Conformation has to be assessed as part of the bigger picture, as it applies to the intended purpose of the horse. Certain conformation faults may render a horse unsuitable for a particular job, such as three-day eventing, but won't impair it from giving a rider great pleasure as an all-rounder. In reality, there have been in the past, and will be in the future, superstar horses with less-than perfect figures. A general rule when assessing conformation is that everything should be in proportion.

The **head** should be in proportion and representative of the type of horse. For instance, an Arabian will have a slightly dished face, while a cob type will have a rounder nose and heavier, less defined outline to the shape of the head.

The **upper and lower jaws** should meet evenly in front, as horses with ill-matched jaws can have feeding problems.

A kind, bright, interested **eye**, well set on the side of the head, is generally accepted as a representation of a similar temperament. An eye with too much white

POINTS OF A HORSE

POLL
FORELOCK
EYE
CHEEK-BONE
NOSTRIL
MUZZLE
CURB GROOVE (BARS)
CREST
THROAT
GULLET
SHOULDER
CHEST
ELBOW
FOREARM
BRISKET
KNEE
CANNON BONE
FETLOCK JOINT
PASTERN
WALL
TENDONS
ERGOT
WITHERS
BACK
LOIN
CROUP
DOCK
HIP JOINT
RIBS
SHEATH
STIFLE
GASKIN
FLANK
CORONET
FOOT
HEEL
HOCK
HAMSTRING

FRONT LEGS AND PASTERNS

  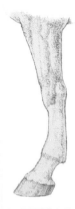

A WELL-CONFORMED FRONT LEG	OVER AT THE KNEE	BACK AT THE KNEE	SHORT, UPRIGHT PASTERN	LONG, SLOPING PASTERN

surrounding it is frequently considered to denote a cheeky, bad-tempered, horse.

Head and neck. The way the head is set onto the neck is important. A horse with a very thick jowl (the area under the jaw) will find it less easy to flex through the jaw and poll (the top of the neck, behind the ears) and will, therefore, find it more difficult to round and soften into a good shape in response to the rider's contact. It will also find it difficult to flex softly into a bend in circles and turns. In a good riding horse, the neck is usually well set on, coming up and out of the wither and tapering to the head, with good muscle above and no obvious bowed muscle underneath, which is representative of a horse with a tendency to hollow its back or of bad training. A good 'length of rein' describes a sufficiently long neck; a short neck can be difficult to round, as can a low set neck. Stallions will have a thicker, more muscular neck than geldings or mares.

Body: The horse's withers should be at an equal height or higher than the croup. A horse said to be 'croup high' will find it more difficult to carry weight on the hindquarters. The withers should be well formed and, together with a good sloping shoulder, will provide a naturally comfortable place for a saddle to sit. A short, upright shoulder may indicate a short, choppy stride.

Chest: It should be deep and broad, providing good room for the internal organs.

BROAD FLAT KNEES

Back and loins: When the horse is looked at from the side, the back should form a rectangle with the legs, and it should look as if a saddle would fit neatly into place in the middle of the back. Mares tend to have longer backs than male horses. A hollow back is considered a weakness or fault, as is a roach back (one with a convex rather than concave slope to the loins). The loins should be well muscled and strong. Anything less is usually a sign of undernourishment or weakness.

The **croup** should slope gently downward towards the dock and be strong and well muscled. At rest, the tail should extend in a natural curve from the croup, but it should be carried proudly when the horse is moving. A clamped tail is often a sign of nerves and tension, whereas a very highly carried tail is a sign of excitement.

A tail carried to one side may be an indication of a back problem.

The **hind limbs and hindquarters** are the horse's 'engine', and their action propels it forward. The whole of the upper hind leg, incorporating the thigh and stifle, should appear strong and powerfully muscled while the thigh should be long and broad.

Hock is a crucial joint in the horse and takes a lot of strain, particularly in collected work, such as advanced dressage, and fast work, such as racing. The hock should be well defined but not fleshy. It should point rearward, not inward (known as cow-hocked), nor should it bow out. When the horse is standing squarely, from the point of the hock down the back of the leg should appear as a vertical line and, ideally, should line up plumb with the outer point of the hindquarters. The hind limbs should appear angled through the hock joint and horses with straight hocks will normally find it more difficult to engage the hind legs under the body.

Cannon bones which make up the leg from knee and hock downward, should appear short to the ground for strength and balance. The term 'clean legs' means that the tendons stand out as clean lines without lumps, bumps or swelling.

Front limbs should appear parallel when viewed from the front. From the side, they should form a vertical line to the ground, which ideally should line up plumb from midway along the top of the shoulder blade, down the middle of the leg and reach the ground at the back of the heels.

BACK LEGS

WELL-FORMED REAR

COW HOCKS WITH POINTS TURNING IN

BOWED (SICKLE) HOCKS WITH TOES TURNING IN

The ideal **elbow** is large, well formed and stands free from the chest wall. Horses that appear 'tied in' in this area will not move freely out of the shoulder on the flat or over fences.

The **knees** should be broad and large when viewed from the front. A small, narrow knee appearing tied in above or below is an indication of weakness. A horse with a natural knee position slightly in advance of the lower limb is known as 'over at the knee' and tends to have a more elastic knee joint than horses with very straight legs. The opposite, known as 'back at the knee' or 'calf-kneed', will put greater strain on tendons.

The **fetlock** should be well shaped and strong, neither puffy nor too rounded. The angle from fetlock to hoof, the pastern, ideally forms a smooth line. Upright pasterns can lead to more concussion in movement, while long pasterns impede steadiness in movement and put extra strain on the tendons. The hind pastern tends to be more flexible than the front pastern. The angle from the pastern through the hoof should be harmonious.

The **hoof** should be constructed of healthy, strong horn and not be brittle or show evidence of cracks or ridges. The frog which is the soft, leathery pad on the underside of the foot, should be healthy

SIDE VIEW OF HINDQUARTERS

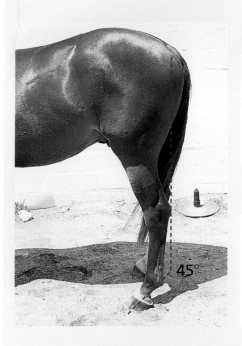

NICELY ROUNDED HINDQUARTERS

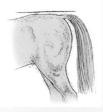

CROUP TOO STRAIGHT
AND TAIL TOO HIGH

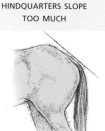

HINDQUARTERS SLOPE
TOO MUCH

HIND LEG IS TOO BENT

HIND LEG IS TOO
STRAIGHT

and surrounded by a defined area of sole. The bars of the hoof and heel should be well defined, as flat feet tend to be weak.

Overall, the **feet** must be appropriate to the size and type of horse and the work it is to perform. Heavier horses will have much larger, broader feet than lighter riding horses. From the front, the feet should appear straight, not pigeon-toed (pin-toed) or splayed out. Boxy, small and upright feet will be more vulnerable to problems, as will feet with an exaggerated slope.

THE HORSE IN ACTION

After assessing the way a horse is put together while standing square (its conformation), the next stage of assessment is based on the way the horse moves, both naturally and with a rider on its back.

From the point of view of the riding horse, the most important aspect is that it moves with clean, true gaits (the natural way of moving) at all times. While a show jumper will be expected to have a good quality canter and an event horse should be able to stretch at a steady gallop, these traits can be developed through good training. Provided the natural gaits are sound in the first place, most horses can be trained to meet special requirements.

The way a horse moves is an indication of its willingness to go forward and is an essential ingredient for both competition and riding horses. Generally, in all gaits the horse should move with energy, rhythm, regularity and elasticity. Transitions between gaits should be smooth, and a well-trained horse should respond instantly to its rider's commands to either increase or decrease speed.

Above: *The trot is a clear two-time rhythm, where the footfalls are made in diagonal pairs (right fore, left hind and left fore, right hind), as this horse shows.*

BREEDS AND TYPES

There are many breeds and types of horses throughout the world. Breeds have developed their characteristics over generations, according to the climate, terrain and conditions of their native land and through their customary use.

Although the horse has served man through the ages as a means of transport in times of war and peace, in agriculture and industry, nowadays, the horse has become part of the leisure industry in many parts of the world, and breeds have had to adapt to the change.

New crosses between breeds, and the introduction of new bloodlines to improve and refine breeds, tell the story of the development of the modern horse.

A breed is technically a strain without the introduction of blood from any other strain. While this criterion may cloud the definition of a 'breed' as opposed to a type (which is determined by the sort of work that a horse does, such as a hunter, for example), the horse world refers constantly to horse breeding, breeding championships, breed societies and so on, so the newcomer should not feel intimidated by such technicalities. Indeed, if we look back over the centuries, most 'breeds' have been influenced, improved

and refined by the injection of 'foreign' bloodlines. Each breed has its own history, but there are two real breeds whose influence surpasses all others, the Arabian and the Thoroughbred.

Although there are never any guarantees, different breeds do have different talents and it is well worth considering the known characteristics of the world's most popular breeds before you buy. There are official breed societies in all countries, and pure-bred horses and ponies will usually be registered with these societies, as well as with the relevant stud books. Generally, registered horses and ponies are more expensive than those that are not registered. If a horse has good breeding, it can command an even higher price. However, when it comes to competitive equestrian sports, the price tag of animals that excel is immediately raised, whether they are registered or not. By the same token, a horse with excellent breeding may sell for next to nothing simply because it has not achieved what it was bred to do.

If you are buying a child's first pony, remember that many children ride unregistered, cross-bred ponies quite happily and with great success.

Left: *Horses come in many colours; however, certain breeds may have their characteristic colours.*
Inset: *The Arabian horse is renowned throughout the world for its purity of breed, elegant lines and exceptional grace.*

AMERICAN QUARTER HORSE

The first all-American breed, the Quarter Horse originated in Virginia, USA, in the early 17th century. It was used as a work horse, pulling wagons and herding cattle. The early settlers used to run horses over quarter-mile races, hence the name. The Quarter Horse was developed from original stock brought to the Americas by the Spanish, together with the addition of Thoroughbred blood imported by the English settlers.

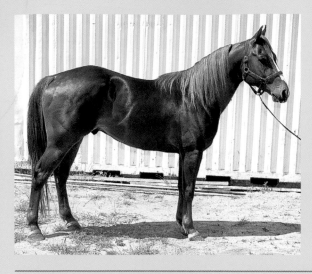

Compact and heavily muscled, the Quarter Horse soon proved its ability in sprint racing. The modern Quarter Horse, which is claimed to be the most popular horse in the world, enjoys widespread popularity, particularly in the USA, where it is used for Western riding, showing, flat racing and general riding. More than three million horses are currently registered with the American Quarter Horse Association.

AMERICAN SADDLEBRED

Developed during the 19th century to provide a comfortable, well-mannered ride for plantation owners in the southern states of the USA, the American Saddlebred (called American Saddlers in some countries) is the best known of the so-called gaited breeds. In addition to a highly elevated walk, trot and canter, these horses are schooled to produce two artificial four-beat gaits, the high stepping 'slow gait', and the extremely fast 'rack'.

Originally evolved from the Narragansett Pacer and Canadian Pacer, an infusion of Thoroughbred, Arabian and Morgan blood gave this horse its eye-catching, proud looks. Popular with enthusiasts as a show horse, the Saddlebred's artificial carriage and gaits are produced by leaving the feet long and shoeing with heavy shoes. These horses are ideal for both pleasure and trail riding.

ANDALUCIAN

While the origin of the Andalucian as a breed is not entirely certain, this Spanish horse has had a great influence on other breeds in Europe, but most particularly in the USA, through its introduction to that continent by the Conquistadors. The Andalucian breed has a strong association with bull fighting in Spain, but in recent years it has begun to enjoy renewed popularity among dressage enthusiasts, especially those interested in the classical high school movements.

Usually, grey, black or bay, the Andalucian is a horse of great presence, with a strong front and proud neck. The temperament is excellent and its natural movement ideally suited to dressage. The emergence of a competitive Spanish dressage team in 1995, with two members mounted on Andalucians, has done much to further the breed's popularity.

ANGLO-ARAB

The Anglo-Arab is a popular riding horse that combines the best of both Arabian and Thoroughbred blood. Originally produced in the UK, Anglo-Arabs are now bred in many other countries where respective stud books have varying requirements, particularly regarding the minimum percentage of Arabian blood allowed. In France, which has the largest breeding programme in the world, horses must have at least 25 per cent Arabian blood to be entered in the official stud book. Arab stallions are put to Thoroughbred mares, and only Anglo-Arab, Arab and Thoroughbred ancestry is permitted. Thoroughbreds primarily provide size, scope and movement, while Arab genes introduce intelligence, soundness, stamina and good temperament. This horse has proven itself in all the Olympic disciplines.

APPALOOSA

In the 18th century the Nez Percé Indians developed a distinctive breed, which they called 'a Palouse horse' after the Palouse Valley of Idaho and Oregon, USA. The term eventually became known as the Appaloosa.

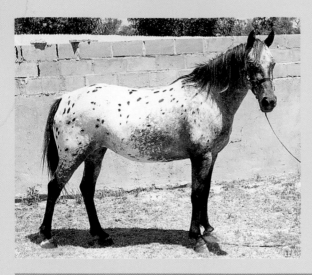

The Indians applied a skillful breeding policy to original Spanish stock, from which evolved a hardy horse of good temperament. Not all painted or spotted horses are Appaloosas, however, and there are five principal coat patterns: blanket – white rump or back spotted with any colour; marble – mottled all over the body; Leopard – spots of any colour or mixed colour on light background; snowflake – white on any colour except grey; and frost – white on a dark background.

In general, the skin is a mottled black and pink and the eye is surrounded by a white sclera. The hooves may be striped and the mane and tail are short and sparse.

ARABIAN

The Arabian is probably the purest breed and is one of the world's oldest and most intelligent horses, boasting a romantic history that has influenced the development of the horse in the modern world. It was developed as a distinct breed by the desert tribes of the Arabian Peninsula. Characteristically, the purebred Arabian should have a small, elegant tapering head with the classical 'dished' face, a broad forehead with prominent large eyes, small ears and a short muzzle with flaring nostrils. The back is shorter, as the Arabian has one vertebra less than other breeds. Its limbs may look more delicate than other breeds but are deceptively tough. Traditionally, the Arabian was a small horse, but newer trends in breeding have succeeded in increasing the height without diminishing the characteristics of the breed.

CAMARGUE

An ancient breed indigenous to the Rhône Delta in the south of France, the famous white horses of the Camargue have been the subject of mystery and legend for hundreds of years and are featured in cave drawings that date back to 15000BC. Somewhat shaggy and wild looking, with a short neck and coarse, heavy head, it is technically a pony since it stands no higher than 1.42m (14hh). They are strong, agile, sure-footed, very courageous, and make excellent mounts. Today they are used in their native land on farms, to work cattle, and in the tourism industry for sight-seeing on horseback. Ironically, although they have been the traditional mount of the French cowboy (or guardian) for centuries, it was only in 1968 that the Camargue was officially recognized as a breed. Registered Camargue horses are branded with a 'C' as a means of identification.

CLEVELAND BAY

Originating from Yorkshire in England, the Cleveland Bay is one of the oldest established British breeds and its history can be traced to the Middle Ages. The breed is derived from the Chapman horse which was bred as a pack horse and was also used by Medieval travelling salesmen (or chapmen). Always bay in colour, with black points, the Cleveland Bay is known for its substance and power. The breed also enjoys something of a unique position as a 'purebred' warm-blood, and for more than a century it has been used to improve many of the European Warmblood breeds. Still popular as a carriage horse, the Cleveland Bay also shows talent in dressage and jumping and has a developed following in Australia, the USA and the UK as a competition horse (either as a purebred or, latterly, crossed with Thoroughbred blood-lines to improve performance).

CONNEMARA

The Connemara pony is the only breed indigenous to Ireland. Its precise origins are not known, but the first ponies are believed to be a mixture of Arab, ancient Barb and Andalucian blood from horses brought into the country by travelling merchants. During the 19th century, imported Arabs bred with these ponies and, in the early 20th century, Welsh Cob stallions were introduced as part of an official breeding programme. The first stallion recorded in the Connemara Stud Book in 1926 was a part Welsh Cob grey out of a native mare. The modern Connemara combines the strength and hardiness of the original mountain pony with the speed, agility and beauty of the Arab. They grow to maximum pony height which is 1.47m (14.2hh) – and are suitable for both adults and children to ride.

DARTMOOR

The Dartmoor Pony originated on the moor of the same name, in the south of England. In the late 18th century, during the Industrial Revolution, Shetland Pony stallions were let loose on the moors in an attempt to produce a cross-breed that would make a good pit pony and the Dartmoor breed virtually disappeared.

In the 1920s, Welsh Mountain Ponies were introduced in an attempt to save the breed and selective breeding programmes were started. When the moors were used for training during World War II, the breed was once again threatened with extinction. Today, the small, hardy Dartmoors are in great demand as riding and jumping ponies and are bred on private studs. The breed is an ideal first pony for children as it is both gentle and small, reaching only 1.27m (12.2hh). They are usually black, brown or bay.

DUTCH WARMBLOOD

The Netherlands has a thriving horse-breeding industry, organized along similar lines to Germany, but falling under one main administration, the KWPN – the Royal Stud book of the Netherlands. Like the other Warmblood breeds, the Dutch Warmblood has been bred to fulfil the need for an outstanding competition sport horse. The official breeding policy of the Dutch Warmblood Society has been to produce 'a noble and likable horse with an honest character'. In the interests of agility, breeders aim for a height of 1.67m (16.2hh). Most are bay or brown in colour.

Over time, the original heavy working and carriage-horse breeds typical of the Netherlands (the Groningen, and the lighter Gelderlander), were combined with English Thoroughbred, and German and French bloodlines to establish the Dutch Warmblood, a riding type and successful sport horse.

EXMOOR

One of the most distinctive of Britain's nine native pony breeds, the Exmoor is believed to have evolved from an ancient wild pony which was small in size (1.22–1.27m/ 12–12.2hh), brown or bay in colour and resistant to wet conditions. Originating from the remote moor of the same name in Somerset, England, it has remained the same for centuries. The Exmoor has a very distinctive jaw formation and evidence of a seventh molar. It has unique hooded eyes, a thick growth of short hair at the top of its tail and a double-textured coat. Used to pull chariots during the Bronze Age, it was later used for hunting and, much more recently, as a child's pony and for driving. The Exmoor is bay, brown or dun, with black points, and a lighter 'mealy' colouring around the eyes, on its muzzle and on the inside of its flanks. Males grow to 1.30m (12.3hh) and females to 1.27m (12.2hh).

FRIESIAN

This is a small, thickset horse bred in the Friesland province of the Netherlands. Always black, these horses traditionally have long flowing manes, feathered (hairy) heels and a high stepping gait.

Friesian horses were introduced to Britain by the Romans, where they formed the basis of the Dales and Fell native pony breeds.

A coldblood descended from one of the founding trio of 'primitive' horses, the thick-legged, heavy-bodied Forest Horse, Friesians excelled in trotting races during the 19th century. Ironically, their popularity in this sport led to interbreeding which eventually threatened the breed. According to a stud book dating from 1879, there were only three Friesian stallions left in Friesland in 1913.

Selective breeding continues today and, in recent years, the good-natured Friesian has enjoyed popularity as a specialist dressage and display horse.

HAFLINGER

The native pony of Austria, the Haflinger is thought by some to have originated from the old-time Alpine Heavy Horse crossed with Arab blood. Certainly its founding sires were Arabian: the principal bloodlines can all be traced back to El Bedavi XXII, a descendant of El Bedavi, an Arabian imported to Austria in the 19th century, and his offspring. Sturdy, with a neat head, Haflingers are always palomino or chestnut in colour with a flaxen mane and tail.

Although only 1.40m (13.3hh) high, Haflingers were originally used as sure-footed mountain pack horses. They are still used for agricultural work and in the forestry industry. Good temperament and an excellent weight-carrying ability have made the Haflinger is a popular leisure pony in many countries of the world, for general riding as well as carriage driving.

HANOVERIAN

In 1736 the first 12 Hanoverian stallions stood at the State Stud at Celle. The Stud, founded the previous year by King George II of England and the Duke of Brunswick, is still the heart of Hanoverian breeding. The original product of the stud was good, hardy horses, easily adaptable for

work on the land or for general riding, and during the 19th century a considerable amount of heavy stock was introduced from Britain. The fortunes of the Hanoverian varied during the early 20th century until the implementation of a revised leisure and sport horse breeding programme introduced the Thoroughbred, Arabian and Trakehner stock that has refined the Hanoverian type into a top quality riding and competition horse.

For the first 40 years or so, most of the stallions came from Holstein, East Prussian, Neapolitan, Andalucian and English Thoroughbred stock.

HOLSTEINER

The district of Schleswig-Holstein in northern Germany is believed to have been a horse breeding area since the early Middle Ages. Its influence extended to areas such as Hanover and neighbouring Denmark.

At one time, Holstein was renowned for breeding fast, big-framed, strong coach horses with a high showy action. To develop the lighter-bodied modern riding type, English Thoroughbreds were used extensively.

This influence, particularly that of Ladykiller and his sons Lord and Landgraf, as well as the Selle Français stallion Cor de la Bryère, has produced many top show jumpers in the past, (and continues to do so), and some exceptional dressage horses. Although not one of the largest breeding areas in Germany, the Holstein district can lay claim to a number of top performance horses, up to Olympic level.

ICELANDIC

Descended from a mixture of horses taken to Iceland by early immigrants, the Icelandic horse has been a pure breed for more than 800 years.

After a disastrous attempt to introduce Eastern blood, in 930AD the government of Iceland made it illegal to import horses. Today, four different types of Icelandic horse can be identified, each distinct in terms of conformation and function. The best-known is the Faxafloi, which is bred in the south west and is very like the Exmoor Pony.

The Icelandic horse stands at between 1.30 and 1.37m (12.3–13.2hh), however, it is never referred to as a pony. There are 15 basic colour types, including piebald, skewbald and other specific combinations.

The native Icelandic horse is distinguishable by five characteristic gaits – the normal walk, trot and fast gallop, and two ancient gaits, the 'pace' and the 'rack' (or tölt).

IRISH SPORT HORSE

The Irish Sport Horse is a leading Warmblood breed which combines Thoroughbred blood with the indigenous Irish Draught horse. Modern-day Irish Draught stallions stand at up to 1.73m (17hh), but by crossing them with Thoroughbred mares, a smaller competition horse can be produced.

The Irish Draught is descended from the great horses of France and Flanders which were imported to Ireland after the Anglo-Norman invasion in the 12th century. These, in turn, were crossed with imported eastern and Andalucian horses to create a draught and riding horse suitable for use on the farms.

Today, the selectively bred Irish Sport Horse combines surefootedness, stamina, athletic ability and an intelli-

gent but sensible temperament with jumping talent. In the past decade, the breed has enjoyed success in international show jumping.

LIPIZZANER

The breed is named after the Lipizza Stud near Trieste, which was founded in 1580 by the Hapsburg Archduke Charles II, son of Emperor Ferdinand I of Austria. The stud, which still exists today as a breeding, riding and tourist centre, hosted the 1993 European Dressage Championships. The Lipizzaner is believed to have originally descended from the Andalucian breed, with the later introduction of Arabian blood. The breed lines of the founding stallions – Maestoso, (a grey horse born in 1819), Siglavy, (a pure-bred grey Arab 1819), Pluto, (a grey horse from Denmark 1765), Conversano, (a black horse from Italy 1767), Favory, (born in 1779) and Neopolitano, (a bay horse 1790) – have been maintained and are found today in all purebred Lipizzaners, including the horses at the internationally renowned Spanish Riding School of Vienna, where the traditions of classical dressage are upheld.

LUSITANO

This showy Portuguese horse probably originated from Andalucian blood and, like its Spanish counterpart, has been associated with mounted bull fighting. An ancient breed, now bred throughout Portugal, it surprisingly only got its name in 1966 (from Lusitania, the old Latin name for Portugal). The physical characteristics and conformation of both the Andalucian and Lusitano are much the same. Most are grey or bay and they have long, thick manes and tails. The Lusitano has great presence, yet it stands at only 1.57m (15.2hh).

The Lusitano is intelligent and agile, and was used at one time by the Portuguese army. Even though it is not built to gallop, these traits make it an ideal horse for herding cattle.

Its grace and showy action makes it particularly suitable for classical dressage. They are now bred for this discipline in Britain, Europe and America.

NEW FOREST PONY

Herds of New Forest Ponies still run and breed free in their native habitat, the New Forest in Hampshire in the south of England, where they have lived since the 11th century, but they also flourish in domesticated conditions.

There is a big variation in the height of New Forest Ponies; those bred in the forest can be as small as 1.22m (12hh), while those bred on stud farms often reach a maximum height of 1.47m (14.2hh). Any coat colour is allowed, except for piebald, skewbald and blue-eyed cream. Most ponies are bay and brown, often with white markings on their heads and legs.

A good-natured all-rounder, the New Forest is popular for pleasure riding and competitions. They have competed successfully in most equestrian activities including jumping, dressage, long-distance riding and even in harness.

OLDENBURG

The original Oldenburg was a heavy coach horse. Count Johann von Oldenburg imported oriental, Spanish and Neapolitan horses in 1580 as foundation stock. His son, Count Anton Günther von Oldenburg, was known as the 'Stable Master of the Holy Roman Empire' for his promotion of horse breeding, which included the establishment of schools where farmers could learn about horse management. The Oldenburg preserved its original characteristics and bloodlines far longer than any other German regions until, after World War II, the demand for lighter riding horses resulted in an injection of Thoroughbred blood. The original type can still be found in some Polish studs, for example, but the modern competition type established itself as a success in a very short time. Apart from the ridden sports, horses from Oldenburg are still used for carriage driving.

SELLE FRANÇAIS

Cheval de Selle Français, or French saddle horse, as the name translates, is a product of the breeding system instigated in 1958, which brought together all the French provincial stud books under one banner. The Selle Français type horse developed originally from the use of Thoroughbred stallions on native mares. Unlike the other Warmbloods, there is also evidence of the use of fast-trotting stock (Norfolk Roadsters) in the early days. Much later there was a significant infusion of Arabian and Anglo-Arab bloodlines. Today most Selle Français horses are sired by Selle Français stallions, and more than half are sired by either Thoroughbreds or Anglo-Arabs.

The Selle Français is a highly successful competition horse that has excelled in international show jumping. A lighter type is also bred for non-Thoroughbred racing.

SHETLAND PONY

One of the smallest breeds in the world, the Shetland has found popularity as a child's pony or driving pony in many parts of the world, far from its native habitat in the Shetland Isles of Scotland.

The hardiness of the Shetland is legendary and its strength is believed to be greater kilo-for-kilo than any other equine breed.

The Shetland Stud Book Society rules that a standard Shetland Pony should not stand more than 107cm (42in) high at four years or older. This is one breed whose height is traditionally measured in inches and, more recently, in centimetres, rather than hands. The breed also has miniature ponies which must not be any bigger than 86cm (34in). They can be of any colour, including mixed colour but excluding spots, although the traditional colours are black and white-grey.

THOROUGHBRED

The Thoroughbred is the noblest of breeds. Prolifically successful in racing, eventing and, to a lesser extent in show jumping; it pervades the horse world through its influence on other breeds. To be eligible to race and to register as a pedigree Thoroughbred, a horse must fulfil the criteria for entry into the General Stud Book, which was founded in 1793 and is currently administered by Weatherby's in England and Ireland. Other countries have associated stud-books and champion Thoroughbreds have been bred in England, Europe, Canada, the USA and New Zealand. The Thoroughbred can be over 142cm (14.2hh) and any solid colour. Alert, sensitive horses with refined, quality looks, they are strong and have great stamina. As a breed, they have excellent freedom of move-ment, enhanced speed, and great powers of recovery from exertion.

TRAKEHNER

The Trakehner has a long history which, despite the influence of war, can be traced back to East Prussia in the 13th century. Modern Trakehner breeding was founded at the Royal Stud set up in 1732 by Friedrich Wilhelm I and expanded over the years via regional satellite studs. After World War II, fewer than 1000 breed-ing horses reached West Germany fol-lowing a gruelling 1300km (800-mile) trek from East Prussia. Although by the mid-1950s the Trakehner Verband, the successor to the East Prussia Stud book, registered fewer than 700 ani-mals, it is now the third largest breed association in Germany, and has been influential in refining the stock of other breeding districts. There is a great deal of Thoroughbred blood in the Trakehner breed, which is typically refined, elegant, free-moving and tending towards the blood horse in temperament.

WALER

Intended for work on the sheep stations in Australia (particularly New South Wales), these horses were bred from the first horses imported into Australia – initially Cape Horses from South Africa and later Thoroughbreds, Arabs and Anglo-Arabs. Although not terribly fast, they

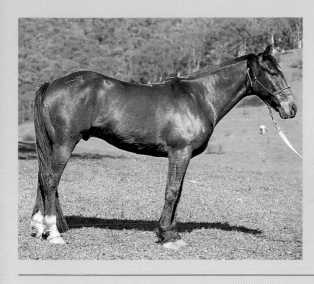

are agile with remarkable stamina, which makes them exceptional working horses. The Waler's successor, the modern Australian Stock Horse, has some Quarter Horse and Percheron blood and the Australian Stock Horse Society is working towards promoting and standardizing the breed.

Walers have good temperaments and a sound constitution, and range in height from 1.52–1.68m (15–16.2hh). Although all-rounders, Walers are known to have great jumping talent: in 1940 one was recorded as jumping 2.54m (8.33ft), which is higher than international A-grade show jumpers are expected to clear.

WELSH COB

For centuries Welsh Cobs have been an integral part of Welsh life, working on farms and pulling carts and carriages. In the days when mounted infantries went to war, they were also used to pull guns and equipment. There are two types of modern Welsh Cob, both of which are descended from the original Welsh Mountain Pony, but which also have characteristics from breeding with trotters and Hackney-type horses. The Welsh Pony of Cob type has a height limit of 1.37m (13.2hh) and is recorded in Section C of the Welsh Pony and Cob Stud Book. Now often the result of a cross between a Section D Cob and a Section A Welsh Mountain Pony, they are particularly good jumpers and are popular for trail riding. Section D Welsh Cobs are taller than 1.37m (13.2hh) with no height limit. Used for general riding and in harness, the Cob is hardy, robust and sound.

WELSH MOUNTAIN PONY

The Welsh Mountain Pony, recorded in Section A of the Welsh Pony and Cob Stud Book, has a height limit of 1.22m (12hh) and is probably the prettiest of all Britain's native ponies. When the infamous English king, Henry VIII ordered the destruction of all horses under 1.32m (13hh), because they were too small to carry the weight of a knight in armour, many escaped into the inaccessible Welsh mountains where they lived for centuries. Since the formation of the Welsh Pony and Cob Society in 1902, breeding has been strictly controlled and the modern Welsh Mountain Pony is regarded as one of the finest foundations for horse breeding.

The Section B ponies were originally a cross between Welsh Mountain Ponies and the smaller of the two Welsh Cobs. However, the demand for good quality children's ponies in the late 1920s led to cross-breeding with an Arab and a Barb stallion.

WESTPHALIAN

Westphalia, in northwest Germany, is the heart of German horse country, and it is here that the State-owned Westphalian National Stud was founded at Warendorf in 1826. The breeding management does not aim to breed specialists, but rather produces versatile sport horses which excel in all disciplines. With this in mind, the Westphalian breeders pride themselves on experimentation through the constant importation of modern and new bloodlines. Conformation, basic paces, riding ability and jumping potential are all important selection points for breeding and a strict stallion policy is enforced.

The Westphalian area boasts more than 100, 000 registered riders and the stud is home of the German National Riding Centre. Many of the horses that have been bred, and that have competed here, have gone on to become international champions.

Above: *Riders come in a variety of shapes, sizes and levels of experience. Finding the right horse to meet your needs and skills may take time, and it is a process that should not be hurried.*

▸ DEVELOPING THE BOND BETWEEN HORSE AND HUMAN ◂

The relationship between people and horses is an enduring one, but dealing with animals is always easier and more enjoyable when you have empathy and understanding. To be able to relate to horses, you need to understand their psychology; in order to anticipate horses' reactions you have to understand how they think and why they behave in certain ways. A good understanding also builds confidence on both sides – human and equine.

When faced with a threatening situation, the horse's natural instinct is one of flight, and therefore its perspective on life is one of vulnerability rather than attack. As humans, how we react and feel in certain situations depends on our upbringing and experience. It is the same with horses, which is why careful early handling and training are so important. We can never expect a horse to go against its natural instinct, that is, never to be frightened or wary –

Above: *The bond between riders and their horses is based on mutual trust and respect. Treat your horse well, and it will be your eager companion on many outrides.*

but with good training we can control these instincts and show the horse, in a positive way, that a particular situation or object need not be feared.

Horses are gregarious herd animals, welcoming the company of other horses, as well as other creature companions and humans. Even domesticated stabled horses establish their own 'pecking order'. Either the stallion at the end of the row calls loudest when feed time is due or, as many top riders report, their retired star kicks the stable door demanding attention first when what it considers as 'its' rider walks into the stableyard in the morning.

It is widely acknowledged that the horse responds best to praise and encouragement from its trainer or rider in order to overcome its natural flight instinct and not be dominated. 'Breaking-in', the term formerly associated with a young horse's first conditioning to carry a rider, has now commonly been replaced with terms such as 'starting', which imply much less the idea of domination. From the disabled child fearlessly enjoying the company of ponies as part of therapy to the most successful of international competitive combinations, a common bond – that of trust and empathy between rider and horse – is being developed.

Above: *Regular grooming, caring and gentle physical contact reinforces the bond between you and your horse.*

‣ MATCHING HORSE AND RIDER ◂

Just as with humans, horses have very different temperaments and characteristics depending on their breeding, talents, and how quickly or slowly they grow up. There is really no such thing as a 'bad-tempered' horse, merely one that has reacted antagonistically to some bad experience. 'Bad horses' are made, not born.

Apart from training the horse properly, to ensure these bad experiences do not occur and leave a negative imprint, it is as important to match the right horse to the right job as it is to match horse to rider. A highly nervous, quick-reacting Thoroughbred will lose confidence with an inexperienced handler just as quickly as the handler will. Similarly, a laid-back, big-framed Cob forced to go fast in a jump-off every week is going to be just as unhappy as its frustrated rider who fails yet again to win a prize. In these situations, it is less an admission of failure than one of common sense to acknowledge that both horse and rider would

Above: *A well-schooled, experienced horse can help a young or inexperienced rider to* ·
gain confidence.

be happier with a partner better suited in temperament, objectives and riding skill.

As a general principle, a young horse needs an experienced rider and a novice rider is better off on a steady, experienced horse. While we should not attribute human emotions to animals, it is correct to surmise that horses can feel emotion, that they can pick up 'vibes' and react to a negative or positive environment. Trust and harmony form the basis of any relationship, and it is the same with horses. When these qualities are present, the relationship between horse and rider is capable of bringing much reward and pleasure.

Above: *Horse and rider should be well matched in size and temperament.*

A HOME FOR YOUR HORSE

Before making the decision to purchase a horse, look at how owning one is going to fit in with your current lifestyle. How much time do you have, and how much money can you afford (this is not a cheap pastime). Where are you going to keep the horse, and who is going to look after it?

If the facilities are available, keeping a horse at home is fine in theory, but horses need and thrive on routine and company. It is not the happiest situation to leave a horse alone all day while its owner is at work. Land and stabling are costly to buy and maintain, so increasingly, boarding horses is the most logical option. Known as livery (or agistment in Australia, boarding in the USA), the arrangements for stabling your horse can take several forms. Full board entails the entire care of the horse being undertaken by the boarding establishment, including exercise if the owner is not around to ride it. Half board usually entails the stable undertaking general stable routine and care, such as mucking out and feeding, with the owner responsible for riding and grooming the horse. Working livery is an

arrangement used in teaching establishments, whereby suitable horses are boarded at a lower rate in return for use in lessons. With DIY livery, only the facilities are rented, while the owner does all the work.

With any boarding arrangement, however, it is essential to clarify the terms and responsibilities before the deal is entered into. Working livery, for example, is not going to be feasible if the owner turns up to ride on a Saturday morning to see the horse being ridden by someone else.

It is important to find an establishment where both you and your horse are going to fit in. A riding school that focuses predominantly on dressage, with the jumps stacked in the corner of the arena, will be a frustrating environment for the keen jumper. Similarly, a rider who enjoys hacking in the company of other riders will miss out on this at a serious competition stable where everyone else is competing in shows every weekend.

As well as all-round suitability, the other criteria involved in finding a good boarding stable are very similar to those that are applied in finding a good riding school.

Left: *A good livery yard will offer supervised stabling facilities, as well as a variety of services.*
Inset: *A spacious, well-fenced field is shared by several horses turned out during the day.*

▶ KEEPING A HORSE ◀

In its natural environment, the horse lives at grass with other horses. For a migratory creature of flight, this regime fits in with its desire to roam and graze freely, meets its social instincts to be part of a herd, and fulfils its need for space to exercise.

For young, growing horses, a free-ranging life in a large field or paddock is essential for healthy physical development – strengthening bones, joints and tendons as well as the muscles and internal organs. In reality, though, full-time 'living out' is not always the most practical solution for the working horse, nor, frequently, for its equally hard-working owner.

The reasons for keeping horses stabled include protection from the extremes of climate, management time, the availability of suitable land, and the need to control and monitor the lifestyle of the performance horse.

TURNING OUT

Certain breeds, notably hardy native ponies, can live out at grass all year round, or at least for part of the year while performing light work such as hacking, provided there is access to a constant water supply and a dry, wind-proof shelter.

As the workload increases, and feeding and work regimes become more controlled, the horse may need to be clipped and kept rugged up, so stabling is the only option. However, some daily turn-out time should be provided for every horse, even if space is restricted. It is not only unnatural for a horse to be confined

Top: *Although natural pasture and open fields are an ideal environment for horses, this is not always convenient for owners. However, stable-kept horses need to be turned out daily for their own wellbeing.*

competition season, when the horse is 'let down' to a lower level of fitness in preparation for a rest.

However, for many top riders, the level of relaxation gained by their horse being turned out for short periods outweighs their fears of knocks or bumps. Also, when the horse is used to a routine, it is less likely to race around wildly. Instead, it will settle to graze after a buck and a roll.

With any horse that finds freedom highly exciting, being turned out with a quieter horse, often an elderly horse or pony that remains unimpressed and does not join in, tends to have a settling effect.

to a stable for 23 hours a day, but turn out is a vital factor in keeping the horse's digestive system and circulation in good order, as well as being conducive to its general wellbeing.

Ideally, turn out should have a social aspect for the horse. The natural urge to create a pecking order requires that groups be set up with forethought to avoid bullying. At a boarding stable with limited paddock space, it often takes a bit of management and effort to ensure your horse is turned out with suitable companions. No-one wants their precious horse to need time off to recover from being kicked in the field!

With valuable performance horses in peak condition, which are likely to burst into real 'whoopee time' when turned loose, it is understandable if turn-out time is limited to sole occupation of one small paddock to prevent injury through high jinks. Some horses, when very fit, are so overjoyed when given a taste of freedom that it is considered only feasible to turn them out after the end of the

Right: *Secure, sturdy fencing around the field will prevent horses from escaping.*

ROUGHING OFF AND BRINGING UP

When a horse is to be turned out for a rest – either full time or to spend days in the field and nights in the stable – a gradual adaptation needs to be followed to avoid upsetting its sensitive digestive system.

Known as 'roughing off' or 'letting down', this involves a gradual reduction in the ration of hard feed, a slow cutting down in the number of rugs worn by the horse in the stable, and a gradual increase in the number of hours the horse spends out, to get it accustomed to the change of lifestyle. Similarly, 'bringing up' involves the gradual introduction of hard feed while the horse is still living in the field, and a slow introduction and build-up of the amount of work. This is often advantageously begun with the horse being ridden at walk while living in the field.

Starting work with a calm, laid-back horse is much easier than with a newly clipped, newly stabled horse that will be relishing the effects of its hard feed and may well prove to be very much on its toes!

Before the horse is fully 'roughed off', its shoes – or at least the hind ones – should be removed (some farriers prefer to leave on the front shoes, especially in the case of brittle feet). When the horse is brought up the shoes will need to be replaced and antiparasite medication administered. This is also a good time for the teeth to be checked and for annual inoculations to be carried out.

Above: *Trees provide valuable shade, as well as shelter from the rain and wind.*

Exercise arenas are a bonus for anyone keeping a horse at home. The simplest type would be a flat, grassed area. Remove all stones before using it to ride on, and top-dress (fertilize) it regularly to encourage good grass growth.

The size of a training arena will depend on the work you do with your horse, but it should be at least 30m x 30m (98ft x 98ft) or the size of a small dressage arena – 20m x 40m (65ft x 130ft). Unfortunately, unless the ground is properly prepared before the grass is planted, the surface can be very hard, particularly for jumping. For this reason, sand arenas are preferred or, better still, sand may be mixed with rubber chips, wood shavings, bark, or a specialized polymer or gel polymer. Before the sand is brought in, the subbase must be properly prepared, preferably by a professional.

A circular lunging ring should be at least 20m (65ft) in diameter. If the ring is too big, it is difficult to work with the horse; if it is too small, it could lead to injury. In any case, lunging should only be carried out by a trained person. Sand arenas are common for lunging, although a layer of sawdust may also be spread thickly around the circular track.

Above: *A standard size dressage arena.*
Top: *A circular, sand lunging arena with a secure post-and-rail fence is an invaluable facility for any stable yard or riding school.*

The most important part of field management is the removal of droppings. Horses are just as migratory in their habits of excreting waste as they are in grazing, and laborious as it might be, removing droppings keeps down the levels of worm and parasite infestation and greatly extends the viability of any field.

The more time the horse is going to spend living in the field, the larger the area required. If horses are living out full time at one location, there should be enough ground for pasture rotation, so that areas can be rested. Pasture or meadowland consists of many different grasses, herbs and other plants. Horses tend to head for areas containing the most succulent grasses, which are then eaten to the roots. If these die away and the less appetizing plants take hold, the paddock becomes what is known as 'horse-sick'. Resting paddocks, or alternating horses with other livestock such as cattle or sheep that have different tastes in plants can alleviate this problem.

A horse-sick paddock will need ploughing and reseeding (which is best done after a soil analysis, and in consultation with an expert body, such as a ministry of agriculture or farmers' association). Paddocks can be rolled and harrowed each year before the grass starts to grow, and 'topped' to discourage the spread of less popular plants.

The ideal paddock has well-drained flat ground, is located away from busy roads or other potential hazards, and has natural boundaries of hedges and trees that give protection from the elements. However, most horse owners have to make the most of what is available and it is worth considering that some of the best race and event horses in the world are raised in New Zealand on hills of escarpment proportions. The vital elements are good fencing and a constant supply of clean, fresh water. Unless your paddock has a natural unpolluted running stream with a pebble bed, a reliable alternative water supply must be provided. A purpose-made trough, sited on ground prepared with a stone and sand-drained area, is a wise investment. Old baths or other insecure stopgaps with potentially sharp edges can be dangerous for horses. Bear in mind that fields without access to the main water supply will entail several daily trips with buckets to ensure the water is fresh and constant.

Left to right: *A clever safety device secures a chain; a slip rail is cheap; a chain secures the gate to a pole.*

FENCING

Horses tend to exercise their freedom to roam at any given opportunity unless they are securely and safely enclosed.

- Fencing of at least 1.2m (4ft) high, with top and bottom spacing, is essential.
- Good post and rail timber, treated to discourage chewing and built with rounded corners for safety, makes an excellent enclosure but can be costly.
- Other fencing materials include plain wire narrowly spaced with strong pillar posts, wire mesh, or special products such as wire that has been reinforced and widened with nylon or strong synthetic material.
- Electric fencing can be used temporarily to cordon off a particular area, but is not reliable as the primary means of enclosing horses.
- Gates should be wide enough to lead horses in and out without any risk of catching them or a handler. A well-secured gate with enough ease of access will allow a handler to lead one horse through the gate while dealing with the fastening, and holding a bucket, as well! Anyone who has struggled in the pouring rain with slip rails, a bucket in one hand and yearling in the other, has learned to appreciate the advantages of a well-hinged gate with good ground clearance and a safety catch.

Note: Barbed wire is extremely dangerous and should never be used to fence in horses.

FIELD SHELTERS

Where natural protection from the elements is not available, a field shelter (run-in shed) should be provided. This is normally a rectangular wooden or metal construction, large enough to accommodate the number of horses that may use it, closed on three sides, with one long side left open to allow easy access. You don't want a narrow entrance where horses might catch themselves when barging in or out.

The open front should be positioned away from the prevailing weather, so that wind and rain do not blow straight in. A straw base should be provided in winter if the inside floor gets muddy or churned up.

If hay is to be provided as food or bedding in the shelter during the winter months, it is often a good idea to build a feed store as an annex to the shelter to avoid frequent trips carrying supplies. Such a store obviously needs to be well secured to prevent the horses from raiding it for extra rations.

Right: *An open-sided field shelter provides refuge from the sun in hot climates.*
Top: *Post-and-rail fencing is attractive and safe.*

Styles of stabling vary from area to area and from country to country. Stabling can comprise anything from timber constructions, to natural stone stables to purpose-built indoor barns.

Whatever the building style or materials used, and however humble or palatial the stabling may look from the exterior, there are several essential factors that need to be applied in order to create a good quality home for a horse.

Ventilation is very important. While the actual temperature in the stable should relate to the ambient temperature, it is protection from draughts and from the elements that keeps horses warm, not central heating. However, in countries that are prone to subzero temperatures, heating systems are often utilized in stables and indoor schools.

Horses are very sensitive to draughts, but they do need a lot of fresh air. In cooler climates or seasons it is easy to maintain the airflow in an outside stable, whereas in barn-type stables, particularly in hotter climates, fans or other supplementary ventilation may be needed to keep fresh air flowing. Airflow is normally enhanced by the high roof clearance required for safety, which should be a minimum of twice the height of the horse's wither.

Every stable should have a window that opens outward and is protected by wooden slats or a metal grille on the inside, so the horse cannot access the glass. Safety (shatter-proof) glass should always be used in stables.

Light should replicate natural daylight as far as possible, with skylights and neon or electric strip lights to enhance this where necessary.

Floors should be nonslip for safety reasons. Concrete floors, for example, should be roughened to facilitate a secure grip as well as drainage. Although it is costly, rubber matting is a good investment. In addition to improving grip, it provides a softer base for bedding and is hygienic, as it can be hosed down regularly and disinfected periodically, such as when a new horse moves in or after illness.

Above: *Regular skipping out prolongs the life of bedding and also improves the horse's general stable environment.*

7:00
- Fill water bucket • First feed
- Muck out and lay day bed
- Brush over horse and pick out feet

9:30
- Skip out • Remove rugs if worn
- Saddle up and exercise
- Fill water bucket on return to stable

12:00
- Groom • Put on day rug
- Fill water bucket
- Second feed
- Refill hay net

16:00
- Pick out feet • Skip out
- Shake up bedding
- Remove day rug and brush horse
- Put on night rug
- Refill water bucket
- Third feed

19:30
- Skip out • Lay night bed
- Refill hay net and water bucket
- Final feed

Last thing
- If you are able to do so, visit stable to ensure that all is well.

The electricity supply must be specially insulated against damp and well secured to prevent horses from getting to any cables or wires. Covered safety switches should be used throughout the yard.

Apart from young stock and mares with foals, for which the communal barn proves an excellent winter management system, horses generally have their own 'rooms' (stables or stalls). Whatever the type of stable – a single unit, an outside yard of individual stables or the indoor 'American barn' style – the horse's actual 'house' is known as a loosebox.

Stalls were formerly utilized extensively for working horses, and this remains the case in some countries where horses are used as farm labour. Stalls are still used in the traditional buildings of the Spanish Riding School of Vienna and the Royal Mews; although for horses spending much of their time in the stable, being tethered in a small stall is far from ideal and the larger loosebox is preferable.

Top: *Daily mucking out helps to keep the stable environment clean, hygienic and pleasant for the horse.*

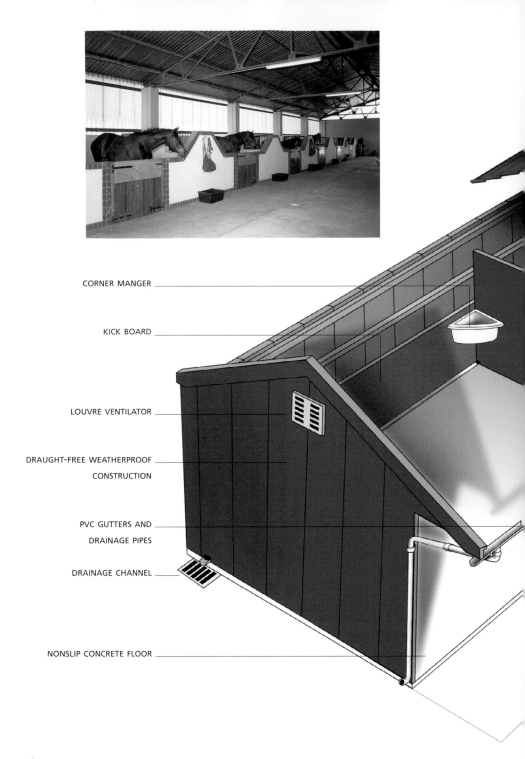

CORNER MANGER

KICK BOARD

LOUVRE VENTILATOR

DRAUGHT-FREE WEATHERPROOF
CONSTRUCTION

PVC GUTTERS AND
DRAINAGE PIPES

DRAINAGE CHANNEL

NONSLIP CONCRETE FLOOR

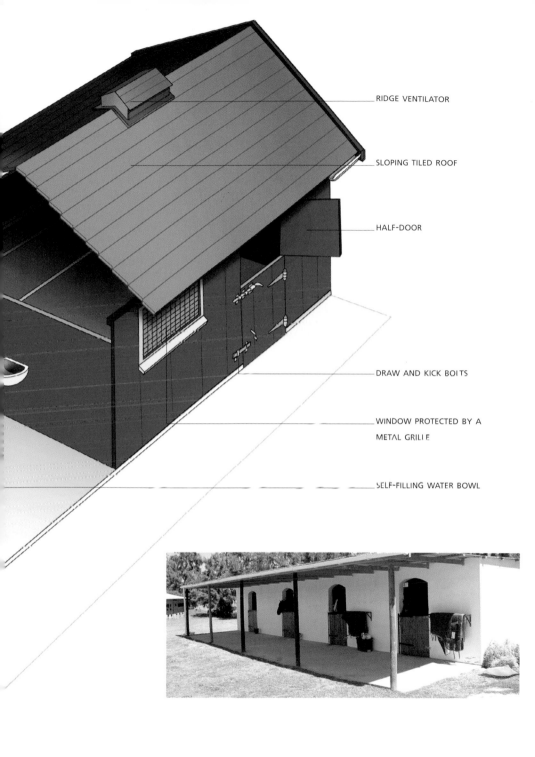

RIDGE VENTILATOR

SLOPING TILED ROOF

HALF-DOOR

DRAW AND KICK BOLTS

WINDOW PROTECTED BY A
METAL GRILLE

SELF-FILLING WATER BOWL

FIXTURES AND FITTINGS

Much care needs to go into the selection of fittings. The principle is rather similar to any situation where there are small children around – try to spot any potential hazards and keep them out of the way.

- **Door catches** need to be secure. Numerous accidents can occur in stables when horses get loose. A door catch at both the top and bottom of the stable door is essential, with the top one a specially designed stable safety latch, so as to avoid inquisitive equine mouths getting caught and injured on it. It is also worth noting that a simple rope clip does not provide a good means of extra security on stable doors, as many horses and ponies have injured themselves trying to undo the rope or by playing with it.

- **Water troughs and mangers** should be situated no lower than the horse's shoulder height, with smooth edges and no protrusions. As a general rule, mangers and water troughs are fitted at the front corners of the stable, away from the door, to ensure that horses that become excited around feed times don't have a chance, however inadvertently, to catch the retreating bearer of the food with a kicking-out heel.
- **Food hatches** enable the food to be delivered from outside the stable into a manger, which then swivels round to be secured in place within the stable. These are increasingly popular, especially in big indoor yards where they save a lot of time previously spent in the opening and closing of doors.
- **Water** must be available as a constant supply, and this just as important in the stable as in the field. Water troughs are situated diagonally across from the manger, but if buckets are used, they are best sited near the door, tucked round the corner to make them less susceptible to being knocked over.
- **Hay** feeding from ground level or from a hay manger is preferable to using hay racks or hay nets, as this helps prevent the ingestion or inhalation of spores and dust. Hay nets, if used, should always be tied with a safety knot and secured by pulling the string to the hay net as high as possible, to avoid a situation where the horse could step on an empty net or get caught up in it.

Above: *A built-in feed trough and hay rack provide a practical feeding facility in a well-lit stable.*

Inset: *A water container can be securely attached to the wall.*

Good bedding is essential for the horse's comfort, as insulation from the cold and for protection as it lies down in the stable. Bedding must also drain well. Choice depends on several factors, but in a busy boarding yard, you should expect to be confined to choosing what the yard uses.

Traditional bedding materials, such as straw and wood shavings, are increasingly being replaced by proprietary products, not only because of the emphasis on making stable environments as dust-free as possible, but also because disposal is becoming more difficult. The days when a muck heap was taken away for free by the local farmer are almost over, and disposal of waste is now a cost that needs to be taken into account by stable managers.

Good quality straw – wheat straw being the optimum – makes excellent bedding, as it provides good drainage, is warm and springy, and is aesthetically pleasing for the owner. The drawbacks are that it is not

always dust-free and can provide too much of an extra snack for the horse.

Wood shavings are absorbent, less likely to be eaten and are easy to manage if droppings are removed regularly. Sawdust is not satisfactory as it gets very damp and, if ingested with hay, has been known to cause colic. In some countries, peat has a certain following as bedding because of its high absorbency, unfortunately disposal thereof can be difficult.

Shredded paper is entirely dust-free and, therefore, popular for horses with dust allergies. Proprietary brands of bedding, made from material such as hemp, are also entirely dust-free and absorbent, but can be expensive, although they are effective when managed correctly with the regular removal of droppings. There is also a variety of commercial straw-based products on the market that are guaranteed to be dust-free.

Above: *Wood shavings are a popular and practical form of bedding that is absorbent.*
Top: *Straw is an economical bedding material that is favoured by many people.*

Above: *Straw bedding is provided for a mare and her newly born foal.*

MAINTENANCE

Routine makes a yard easy to run and also pleases its occupants (see p61). Horses thrive on routine. A typical day in the stables starts with feeding, and revolves around feeding at regular times. Fresh water should be made available before each feed, after which the water buckets are removed and rinsed out.

Mucking out takes place after the first feed of the day. This involves the removal of all droppings and wet patches and the addition of replacement bedding. During mucking out, it is best to tie up the horse securely in the stable, as wheelbarrows, parked however flush in the doorway, have been used as jumps during bids for freedom. Once the horse's rugs have been straightened or removed for the day, and hay has been distributed, a fresh bucket of water can be put in place.

Feed mangers should be cleaned daily (would you want to eat from a dirty plate?) and the yard swept tidy after mucking out, once again before the lunch break as well as at the end of the day. This prevents the yard from becoming too dirty.

Tools and equipment should be put away carefully after use, not only for their preservation but also to ensure that they do not become safety hazards.

Skipping out (the process of removing droppings and wet bedding) should be carried out whenever possible. This does save time on the once-a-day big muck out and also saves on the cost of bedding. Stables or stalls should definitely be skipped out before the evening feed and fresh water provided

---

DISPOSING OF MANURE AND BEDDING

You may be able to organize for manure and soiled bedding to be removed from the stables regularly, or find a way to dispose of it yourself. If you live on a farm or smallholding and have the space to keep it while it decomposes, then horse manure may be kept for use in garden beds. Rather than make manure heaps, dig several holes at least 2m x 2m (6ft 6in x 6ft 6in) square and 2m (6ft 6in) deep. Throw the dung inside, together with raw fruit and vegetable waste if you wish. Once the first hole is full, leave the manure to settle and decompose while the vegetable matter rots. By the time the third or fourth hole is full you can probably start using – or perhaps even selling – the first batch. Be sure to locate manure pits away from the house and stables to avoid any odour or flies. Also, make certain that you are not violating any health regulations.

Bedding is a little more difficult to dispose of, although straw can be used as garden mulch or burnt when it dries out. Other types may be dug into the soil or used as fill, provided you do not immediately plan to use the ground for pasture.

Every morning, remove all soiled bedding material and the inevitable piles of manure. Unless you are using the deep litter system (a permanent bed that is cleaned and added to daily, but not mucked out), turn all material methodically to uncover sodden areas as well as any manure that may be hidden underneath.

Sweep the floor clean with a hard-bristled broom. From time to time you should also give the floor a good scrub with disinfectant. After sweeping and/or scrubbing, leave the bedding on the sides and allow the stable to air. Ideally, the cleaned stable should be aired all day, although this will not be possible if the horse lives in.

Move all remaining bedding to the back and sides of the stable, as far as possible separating clean straw or shavings from slightly soiled material. Use a fork and/or shovel to do this, and expose as much of the floor as you can. Scrape away any residue with the sides of the shovel.

Later, spread the slightly soiled material across the floor and cover it with the clean bedding, raking to ensure the floor is evenly covered. Top with fresh straw or shavings if necessary. When laying straw, remember to shake the stalks well to separate them and ensure a nice, springy bed.

▶ TRANSPORTING YOUR HORSE ◀

Transporting horses requires care and experience. It is an exacting task that needs to be tackled properly and responsibly. You may decide to hire a reputable horse transport service, which will provide an experienced driver, but if you decide to transport your horse yourself, be aware of the pitfalls of travelling too fast, and practise with an empty horsebox to get the feel of towing. Although accidents do happen, the best advice is to be prepared and forever careful. You may never have to transport a horse yourself, but the reality is that a huge number of horses and ponies do travel in a horsebox or trailer at some time in their lives, many of them frequently. For instance, your horse will probably have to be moved from its previous owner to the stables where you will keep him. Competitive riders, and those who hunt or participate in endurance events, trail riding, polo, polocrosse and so on, need to get their mounts to the competition venues. Even if you only ride for fun (known as hacking) you may want a change of scenery from time to time – perhaps a ride along a nearby beach. Finally, in the event of illness or injury, the

Above: *A well-trained horse will walk into the horsebox or trailer without any problems.*

horse may also need to be transported to a veterinary hospital.

Ponies and horses that are imported or exported will travel by air or sea. Even though the travel conditions are different, preparation and care remain much the same as for road travel, which is certainly the most common form of transportation. You can either tow a trailer (confusingly referred to as a horsebox in some countries) or you can opt for a larger one-piece horsebox (also called a truck, van or float, depending on where you live).

You will, of course, also need suitable travel equipment, including:

- a head collar
- travel boots
- tail guard and possibly a poll guard for the head
- a rug for the horse
- food and water for the horse, if the trip is to be a long one.

Right: *This luxurious truck has a built-in tack cupboard for added convenience.*
Top: *A large truck can be used to transport as many as six horses at a time.*

LOADING

If you can lead your horse without any problems, there is no reason why you should not be able to load him successfully. Start by positioning yourself a few metres from the ramp and then, looking straight ahead and keeping abreast of his shoulder, walk directly up the ramp with him. If he does not follow willingly, do not be tempted to tug or pull. Instead, talk to him quietly in an encouraging tone and try to keep moving forward, however slowly. Try not to turn his head around and start again, as you will then have lost ground. Keep him facing the horsebox and do not turn away. If the horse stops or hesitates, it is sometimes helpful to encourage him by putting one of his front feet on the ramp for him and then pushing gently from behind. Coaxing with feed may also help, although perhaps a sharp tap with a crop may be more effective. Loading horses can be problematic, particularly if you are inexperienced or

Above: *Horseboxes (trailers) are lined up at a show.*
Top: *A horse is led quietly into a horsebox without any problems.*

unsure of yourself. Horses are sensitive creatures that will take advantage of your insecurity before you even realize it.

A method that often works for difficult animals is to tie a rope or lead to the side of the box – to the pins that secure the ramp – and ask a helper to bring this around the horse's buttocks to persuade him to move forward. A second lead, tied to the other side, will be even more effective. You will need two helpers and they will cross the two leads behind the horse, preventing him from running or pushing out. Be careful as some horses kick out or rear if they become stressed in this situation.

You should never attempt to ride a horse into the box, but for safety you should use a bridle if the going gets rough. You can also try putting another, more willing horse into the box first. Stand nearby with your horse and lead him in once the first animal is inside.

In extreme cases, when a horse consistently refuses to box, possibly because of past trauma, you may need professional assistance. It may take weeks or even months of regularly putting a wary horse in and out of the box at home, with help, before you and the horse can load confidently. Never resort to beating the animal. Wear gloves to avoid rope burns.

When offloading, you or a helper should always untie and then hold the horse securely in the box while someone else opens the ramp and guides him backwards (or forwards if you have a front ramp). Push his hindquarters gently to move him to the centre of the ramp so that he does not slip sideways over the edge and hurt his legs. Some horses run out so you should be ready for this, especially when transporting a horse you do not know.

TRAVELLING WITH A HORSE

Before you transport a horse yourself, take a ride in a horsebox so that you can feel what it is like. In most countries it is unlawful for people to travel in a trailer on public roads, but even a short trip along a farm road or somewhere off the beaten track will give you a good idea of what the horse must endure.

Once on the road with the horse, try to maintain a smooth, steady pace. Avoid sudden braking or accelerating and go around corners slowly. Reduce speed if the road is bumpy. On the open road, build up speed and slow down gradually. Check the box regularly to ensure the horse is safe.

Horses will usually travel happily for four or five hours. If the journey is to take longer, break it to check and water the horses.

Right: *Two horses are transported in a horsebox towed by an ordinary domestic vehicle. The gap between the ramp and roof allows a healthy circulation of air.*

YOUR HORSE'S NUTRITIONAL NEEDS

All horses need fibre, protein, carbohydrates, fats, certain minerals, trace elements and vitamins, although different types of horses and ponies will thrive on different combinations.

While fibre is found in bulk foods, protein is found in the essential amino acids of most cereals, particularly oats, as well as in most other foodstuffs, including lucerne or alfalfa. Proprietary concentrates and custom-mixed feeds contain a controlled percentage of protein and can usually be relied on to provide what is required for good growth Too much protein can be harmful as it overworks the kidneys, but a lack of protein results in poor condition, lack of appetite and possibly inadequate performance.

Carbohydrates provide energy and fuel for growth. They are found in various foods, including grasses, cereals (grains) and concentrated feeds, as well as in molasses, which is sometimes included in the diet. It is important to have the correct balance of carbohydrates and exercise: too much carbohydrates with too little exercise will result in an overweight horse, while too little carbohydrates will lead to a loss of energy, particularly if you are working the horse hard.

Fat regulates body temperature and keeps the horse's skin and coat healthy. Most concentrates contain a small amount of oil and it is not usually necessary to add more. Too much cod liver oil can be harmful as it causes an imbalance the vitamin and mineral content of the diet. If you decide to add oil to meal, use no more than a tablespoon of cod liver oil a day, or add up to half a cup of vegetable oil to the feed daily. Do not add oil to cubes or pellets.

While some minerals and vitamins are present in various types of forage, an unhealthy horse may benefit from supplementation. If the diet is properly controlled, however, vitamins rarely need to be given as a supplement on their own. For instance, although Vitamin A may be given to a horse with dry, cracked hooves and a dull coat, it is freely available as carotene in foods such as carrots, grass,

Left: *Horses love apples, and children love to feed them. This Appaloosa is no exception.*
Inset: *Even if some grazing is available, it is necessary to provide additional fibre and roughage.*

maize (corn) and lucerne (also known as alfalfa in some parts of the world). Vitamin B, which is needed for a sound nervous system, is seldom lacking if the horse is well fed. Vitamin C, found in grass, is produced in the horse's digestive tract and does not usually need to be supplemented. Vitamin D and the minerals calcium and phosphorous are vital for healthy bone development. Phosphorous is plentiful in cereals (grains), and both molasses and lucerne are high in calcium. Magnesium is also essential for good bone structure and as an enzyme activator, while sulphur is needed to produce enzymes, hormones and amino acids. If a horse's diet is well balanced, the body will produce its own Vitamin D by synthesis from the sun's rays. Vitamin E, abundant in sprouting grains, improves the reproductive function of stallions and, to a lesser extent, mares. Vitamin K, also found in sprouting grains and grass, is essential for healthy blood clotting.

Vitamins A, D, E and K are stored in the body fat, while Vitamins B and C are water soluble and required daily. With a good, balanced diet, Vitamins B and C will be produced naturally by bacterial action in the horse's gut.

▶ FEEDING ◀

The horse has a complicated digestive system, including an intestinal canal approximately 30m (98ft) long. This convoluted system is prone to blockages and colic problems if not kept in good working order. In the wild, horses graze constantly, and this 'little and often' process has to be compensated for in the stabled horse. The horse takes up its food with its lips and tongue, and the incisor teeth pull up grass and hay, but the careful process of chewing food is carried out further back by the cheek teeth.

Horses grind their food, which is why the teeth, which continue to grow throughout the horse's life, should be kept in good order. If for any reason they are not, regular checks by a veterinarian or specialized equine dentist will ensure that any rough or sharp edges or hooks are dealt with before they interfere with the chewing process.

To keep its digestive system working properly, it is essential that the horse has access

Right: *Fresh grass provides naturally succulent and nutritious food.*

THE HORSE'S DIGESTIVE SYSTEM

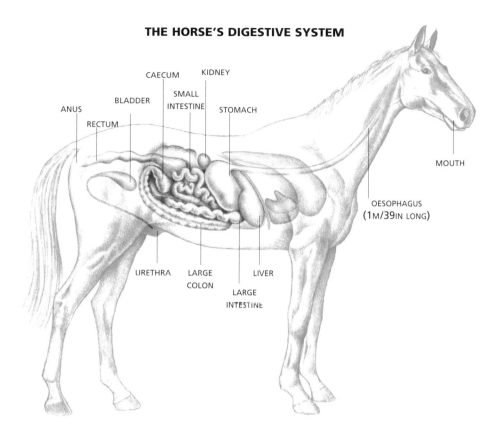

CAECUM · KIDNEY · SMALL INTESTINE · BLADDER · STOMACH · ANUS · RECTUM · MOUTH · OESOPHAGUS (1M/39IN LONG) · URETHRA · LARGE COLON · LIVER · LARGE INTESTINE

to bulk roughage In the form of hay, a hay replacement (haylage), or grass. Nutritionally, a healthy horse is one that has a balanced diet that incorporates the recommended levels of energy, protein, minerals, vitamins and fibre for the work required of it. This should be reflected in the horse's performance and appearance.

A healthy horse should be neither too fat nor too thin, and the coat should not be rough but have a soft, shiny appearance. A horse should always perform willingly at the level consistent with its training.

Right: *When it comes to grazing, the grass is always greener on the other side for some horses.*

THE FOUR MAIN TYPES OF FOODSTUFFS

• Green succulent food: grass, natural pasture
• Forage: hay or hay replacement such as haylage
• Individual cereals (grains): oats, barley, maize (corn), wheat, linseed, bran, sugar beet pulp
• Compound foods (concentrates): mixes, cubes

A horse needs a combination of all these categories, plus vitamin and mineral supplements, to ensure a balanced diet.

FEEDING INGREDIENTS

1. Whole maize (corn) kernels
2. Green pellets (lucerne pellets)
3. Fibre pellets
4. Soyabean meal
5. Crushed maize (corn)
6. Oats

7. Barley
8. Linseed
9. Chaff
10. Bran
11. Molasses

FORAGE

Hay should be available for the horse at least twice a day, morning and night. The horse in light work can be fed hay as required, but for the performance horse in training, the digestive system should contain as little bulk as possible, necessitating an increase in concentrated food.

Dusty hay should not be fed, as the spores found in dusty hay can cause severe respiratory disease if inhaled over any length of time. If hay containing any element of dustiness has to be fed, the slices (flakes) should be pulled apart and soaked fully for 20 minutes to wash out the dust spores. Any spores that are not washed away after this time will expand and be ingested by the horse and not inhaled. In areas where hay quality is not good, for example, in late-cut crops, commercially branded hay substitutes can be used, with a compensatory adjustment to the concentrate ration, as these products are usually higher in protein and energy values.

Hay or forage should never be eliminated from the horse's diet, and owners should not feed more concentrates to replace hay, as this may well disrupt the digestive system.

Right: *A hay net keeps fodder dry and contained.*
Top: *Horses should be fed fodder in the stable, even if they are put out to grass during the day.*

HAYLAGE

STRAW

LUCERNE/ALFALFA

OAT GRASS

Above: *A coarse meal mix, ready to eat.*

CONCENTRATES (CUBES OR MIXES)

The old tradition of feeding a mixture of oats and barley or some other combination of individual cereals (grains) has largely been overtaken by the development of cubes and mixes. These products have an added viability for the one-horse owner, in that a complete food can be bought by the bag, so no storage is needed and freshness can be ensured. They are also useful in large stables where mixing a number of individual 'recipes' is time-consuming.

Cubes: In the wild, horses eat a variety of grasses and very little else, yet cubes are sometimes perceived as being too plain and owners believe the horse will become bored. The domesticated horse, in truth, will not become bored from eating cubes if that is all it knows; it can't miss what it doesn't know. If bought from a reputable manufacturer, cubes will contain only quality ingredients. Cubes tend to have high fibre and low starch levels, making them ideal for hyperactive horses. The ingredients in cubes are thoroughly ground by the pelleting process and have been fully cooked, so no stress is placed on the digestive system. They are also effective in putting weight on the horse when required.

Mixes: At least one major feed manufacturer claims that coarse cereal mixes are designed solely for the horse owner, on the basis that if he or she does not like a particular feed (a preference usually determined by smell and appearance alone), it will not be fed to the horse! Mixes smell better than cubes due to their higher molasses level. Many feed companies now add herbs to the product, to appeal first of all to the owner. The main ingredients of a mix are easily visible – bright yellow flakes of maize (corn) , the green of peas and the golden grains of barley, wheat and, in higher energy mixes, oats.

Low-energy mixes will contain some pellets in the form of fibre pellets (pale brown), and grass or alfalfa pellets (green). These green pellets are often quite sour and can be left in the manger once the horse has picked out the cereal grains. For many horses they are an acquired taste.

COMPOUND FEEDS

These may contain both cooked and uncooked cereals (grains). Although many countries still use uncooked cereals (grains) in their mixes, the horse's digestive system is not able to break down and utilize the starch from these cereals (grains) as efficiently as it can the starch from cooked cereals (grains). It is rather similar to the difference we would experience from eating a raw potato and a baked (jacket) potato.

Cereals (grains) such as barley, wheat, maize (corn), and peas will have been cooked by one of several methods. These are usually described on the packaging and literature as: steam flaking, which is exactly as described; micronizing, where the cereal is passed under infrared lamps while on a vibrating belt (rather like microwaving); extruding, where the whole of the starch structure is broken down with heat and pressure, then reformed; or uncooked, usually applied to oats, which are not cooked as the starch they contain is easily broken down by the horse's gut.

Above: *Oat grass makes a tasty snack at any time.*

CHAFFS AND CHOPS

Chaffs and chops are traditionally fed to horses that are prone to bolting their feed (eating too quickly). Dried grass chaff is a natural product which has the goodness of spring grass that has been cut and the moisture removed. Chaff is very dry, making it difficult for the horse to produce enough saliva to swallow the food with ease.

Chaffs and chops are an additional source of forage or bulk feed, but if fed, the horse's diet should also contain a nutritious element to enable a cost-effective reduction in the hard feed ration. Chaffs were originally just oat straw, cut daily with a chaff cutter. Over time, a niche market appeared, dictated by the needs of the one-horse owner, and now there are many varieties of ready-prepared chaffs available, including molassed, honey, oil and herbal chaffs, plus dried grass and alfalfa.

FEEDING IN HOT COUNTRIES

In a hot country, cubes are a good choice of feed as they remain fresher for longer than mixes. This is due to the lower molasses levels. (A highly molassed product is more prone to mould than a lower molassed product, as molasses is 65 per cent sugar.)

In some warm, wet countries mixes are prone to mites – small insects that can infest a feed store very quickly. These very tiny (pin prick) white creatures move en masse and can cover a large area in a small space of time. There is a distinctive sweet smell to mite-infested feed and the horse will not eat it. Some people are allergic to mites and are able to detect them by streaming eyes and noses.

In hot, humid climates, salt intake will increase. Salt is often mixed with minerals, trace minerals and protein supplements and can be fed by adding it as a top dressing at feeding time, or as a home-made granular lick given ad lib (as required). Commercial compacted salt blocks are also available.

FEEDING FOR BEGINNERS

With an inexperienced owner and a new horse, it is always wiser to aim for a low-energy feed – if necessary, lower than the work required of the horse. If the horse is new to the beginner, the last thing he/she wants is for the horse to be alert and frisky, and the rider on the ground! It is better for the rider to gain confidence by riding the horse calmly, rather than lose confidence by having to hang on. For this purpose, a Horse and Pony Cube or a Cool Mix would be the most appropriate feed. Once horse and rider have established a relationship, the rider has gained confidence and the horse has settled into its new surroundings, a higher energy feed can be provided as required.

Top: *In a large stable, mixing the correct feeds for each horse is part of the daily routine.*

CALCULATING AMOUNTS TO FEED

Especially for those new to horse-owning and feeding, the big feed manufacturers such as Spillers in the UK and Montana Pride in the USA, provide informative literature and run advice lines where queries are answered by a qualified equine nutritionist, so you are well informed on what seems a complex and scientific subject.

The advantages of buying ready-mixed compound feeds are:
• consistency; each batch is analyzed for content
• constant availability of the different types of food required for various activities
• balanced nutritional values; there is absolutely no need to feed extra supplements, as you would to balance straight cereals (grains)

• although more expensive, compound feeds are simple for the novice owner to use. All you have to do is weigh the correct amount.

Your feed room should contain these essentials:
• a spring balance (scale) for weighing hay nets and feed
• a weight tape to put around the horse's girth to assess its weight weekly (see p169)
• a scoop, preferably jug-shaped rather than round (the jug shape's smaller surface area provides a more accurate measure).

Measure a scoop of each feed you use, weigh it and record the weight so you have an accurate record of the weight of each food type

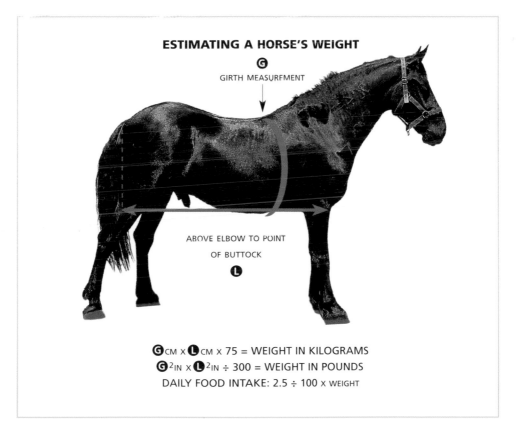

ESTIMATING A HORSE'S WEIGHT

G
GIRTH MEASUREMENT

ABOVE ELBOW TO POINT
OF BUTTOCK
L

G CM x **L** CM x 75 = WEIGHT IN KILOGRAMS
G ^{2} IN x **L** ^{2} IN ÷ 300 = WEIGHT IN POUNDS
DAILY FOOD INTAKE: 2.5 ÷ 100 x WEIGHT

Above: *All horses appreciate a special vegetable or fruit treat such as carrots or apples. These stable mates are waiting for theirs in eager anticipation.*

FEEDING TO SUIT THE WORKLOAD

When choosing a compound feed, always buy a product appropriate for the level of work. Do not buy a competition mix, for example, if the horse is only hacking lightly. If you are feeding a low-energy mix or cube and the horse needs more energy, do not increase the levels of your current feed, rather change to a higher energy feed. If you merely increase the level of feed, you can put more stress on the digestive system without creating the desired result. If the horse needs to carry more weight, choose a conditioning feed designed for the purpose of weight gain rather than more of the current feed.

FEEDING THE PERFORMANCE HORSE

The competition feeds on the market all depend on content, not feeding extra amounts, for effectiveness. They are based on high-energy fibre, unlike traditional cereal (grain) mixes, which are based on high-energy starch. With the new feeds, the high energy comes in a slow release rather than instant form, thus promoting stamina in the performance horse.

High-energy chaffs are essential fibre sources. Oil, in a compound feed, is an excellent form of energy for a horse as it has three times the calories of cereals (grains), is a slow-release energy and provides condition.

Above: *Clinton, a six-year-old Holstein, is a healthy, sound horse, which is the ultimate goal of all horse owners.*

▶ HOW TO FEED YOUR HORSE ◀

The first step is to establish a routine. Horses are creatures of habit and will anticipate meal times according to the clock. It is ideal to feed three or four times a day, although this is not always practical, particularly if you are working and do not have the assistance of a groom. You need to feed at least every morning and every evening, and ensure that the horse has grass to graze and/or some other kind of bulk food in a hay net or manger if he is stabled, or in a hay net or feeding bin if he is in the paddock.

Mix the feed in a suitable feed container before taking it to the horse. Keep a suitable scoop in the feed room, having established what each scoop weighs and how many scoops you should give. Mix everything together and moisten it slightly if giving dry foods, particularly if fine bran is included. Make sure the horse has drunk water before you feed, then top up all water buckets or troughs in the stable and paddock before you leave.

Never feed a horse directly before or after exercise. Wait at least an hour before riding, and cool the horse down by walking for a short while after a ride. Then give him water and a hay net and wait until his pulse and respiration are back to normal and he stops sweating – feel under the chest to ensure he is no longer hot before feeding him.

Top: *Horses should be encouraged to drink water before they are fed.*

Ideally, you need a separate feed room large enough to store all forms of forage: concentrates, any individual cereals (grains) used, supplements and a reasonable supply of fodder – hay, lucerne or alfalfa, and so on. Fodder should be stacked on pallets away from the floor to keep it dry. The room must be dry, cool and clean and should house bins, drums and any other suitable containers that can be securely closed.

You will need several bins that can be sealed in order to decant different types of feed. It is important to finish old feed before decanting new provisions. Moulded plastic is a good material, unlike most paper or hessian bags, which are

easily chewed through by rodents. However careful and clean you are, rats and mice are attracted to hay, straw and lucerne, which is why so many cats are gainfully employed at stables all over the world.

Ensure that, if a horse gets into the feed room, he cannot tip the bins over or knock off the lids. A horse can get a fatal dose of colic if he overeats – this has been known to happen to horses that have managed to enter a feed room.

Above left: *Oat hay and lucerne/alfalfa bales are neatly stacked in a feed room.*
Above right: *Feed is safely stored in a big bin and in smaller barrels.*

GROOMING SKILLS

Every horse is entitled to the minimum of care necessary to enable it to function. The majority of horse owners go much further than this, spending a great deal of effort, and often money, to ensure that their animal is maintained and looked after in the best way possible. Grooming, feeding and caring for your horse takes time and commitment, but as any horse owner will confirm, the rewards more than make up for it.

Grooming is essential for maintaining a healthy coat and skin – it is more than just a cosmetic process. In the wild, horses are 'groomed' by companions in their herd. You can observe horses in the field scratching each other and, on their own, rolling and scratching themselves to remove mud and dust as well as scurf, sweat and loose hair, which in combination with the massage action promotes circulation as well as cell and coat renewal.

In the wild, grooming is an enjoyable process for the horse as it includes relaxation and helps it to 'bond' with its companions. The domesticated horse needs man to take over that role and task. Even in a busy stable where handlers have several horses to groom every day, the grooming period is a chance for a pat and stroke, in addition to some affectionate words. For young horses, physical contact is an important part of the process of getting to know and trust their new herd leader, the human.

New riders will find that grooming is a good way to get to know horses and build confidence in being around them While the length of time required for this process will vary according to the individual handler and horse, an experienced groom will take from 10 minutes for a quick brush-up to up to an hour for a full groom and trimming session.

The horse should be lightly brushed off and tidied before exercise. This provides an opportunity to check the horse over before riding. The main grooming session should come after exercise, to remove sweat and dirt and to generally make the horse comfortable before it is returned to the stable.

Left: *Currycombs are used to loosen sweat and other dirt from the horse's coat, but are not used on the mane and tail.*
Inset: *Regular and thorough grooming is essential for maintaining the horse's coat and skin in peak condition.*

Ideally, grooming should be carried out in a separate area, not in the stable. This ensures that dust does not clog the horse's habitat and also usually ensures more light for the groom.

The horse should be secured with a head collar and rope. Cross ties are the ideal – the horse is secured with two ropes, one on either side, attached to two points in a corridor or grooming box. These allow the handler equal access to both sides of the horse, and a mischievous horse cannot turn round and 'groom' its handler (i.e. nip him or her!). If this is not an option, then the horse should be tied securely using about half a metre's (about 20in) length of rope to avoid too much moving around. All ropes and ties used in stables should be purpose designed, with easily released knots or clip fastenings, in case the horse is startled and pulls back. They should never be attached directly to a hook or wall ring. Wall rings are more safely utilized if a piece of twine or string is attached to the ring itself and the rope is then tied to this. If the horse pulls back hard, the twine will break easily whereas a wall ring won't give way, and the horse could hurt itself or its handler.

GROOMING KIT

1. Rubber currycomb
2. Body brush with sponge
3. Body brush
4. Water brush
5. Hoof scraper
6. Metal currycomb
7. Mane and tail combs
8. Stable rubber (rag)
9. Hoof pick
10. Sweat scraper

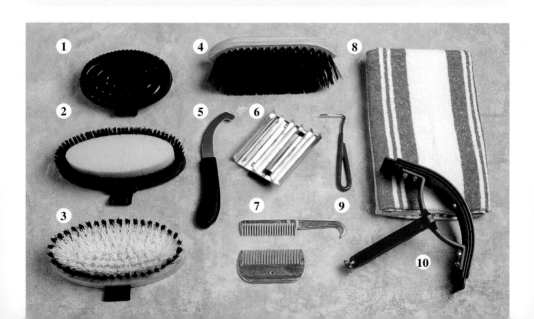

The Feet

The first task is to pick out the horse's feet in turn. With your inside hand, hold the hoof in a supporting grip around the base, near the coronet area, and use the pick to remove any bedding or mud, working from the heel to the toe, taking care when clearing the cleft of the frog (see illustration p101), as this is a sensitive area.

Picking out the feet not only helps to keep a yard tidy, it is also an opportunity to check that the foot is healthy and that shoes are secure before and after exercise. A skip should be placed in position to catch foot debris.

After exercise, the feet can be hosed clean or, if this is not practical, scrubbed lightly using a water brush and a bucket of warm water. Care should always be taken that the heels are thoroughly dried.

The Coat

The grooming process should not strip the coat of its natural oils. In many big training stables, horses are rinsed down after exercise. Excess moisture is removed with a sweat scraper and the horse is then dried off under sun lamps, which promotes relaxed and warmed muscles, before being groomed later. While this is a refreshing process, it is usually only practical in an indoor yard with these special facilities.

A patent shampoo can be used to wash the horse once in a while, such as before a show, but sustained use can strip the coat of its natural lubrication.

Washing a horse outdoors is to be avoided in anything but mild weather, even if it is walked around and allowed to dry under a sweat rug, as cold draughts can cause chills. In warm, sunny climates the horse should still be walked while the coat dries, as horses tend to roll when put back in the stable with a damp coat, thus defeating the object of the exercise.

Generally, the grooming process begins with the removal of sweat and mud, starting at the top of the horse's head and working down. When working on the left side of the horse, the brush should be held in the left hand, and vice versa.

Right: *A rubber currycomb is used to remove sweat and mud from the horse's coat.*
Top: *Picking out the feet removes mud and debris.*

When working on the hind end of the animal, it is helpful to grasp the tail in your alternate hand. It not only avoids a potentially painful swish in your face, but it also discourages a ticklish horse from kicking out.

A rubber currycomb is the most effective tool for removing mud, dust and caked sweat. It is used in a circular, massaging motion (never scrubbing) on the soft parts of the body. It should never be used for the bony head or lower legs, rather use a softer dandy brush for these areas of the horse's body.

Once the worst dirt has been removed, the main massage process can begin. A body brush is used in short but sweeping strokes over the muscles. After every few sweeps, swipe the brush over the metal currycomb (held in your free hand) to keep the bristles free from accumulating dust and loose hairs. Tap the currycomb periodically on the floor to remove the dust. Areas such as under the belly, under the mane and between the legs should not be forgotten.

The Head

When each side of the horse has been brushed, the head needs special care.

Release the head collar and re-attach it so it rests around the horse's neck only. Put the currycomb aside and with one hand held over the bony part of the horse's nose, gently work the body brush around the head, taking special care around the ears, eyes and under the forelock. Work on

Above: *A sweat scraper is used to remove excess sweat, or water after washing.*
Top right: *In warm weather, horses may enjoy a hosing down, but they must be allowed to dry thoroughly to ensure that they do not catch a chill.*

one side at a time, not from the front and be aware that one inconsiderate bang with the hard part of a brush can make a horse fearful and head-shy. On the other hand, gentle brushing can be both calming and enjoyable for the horse.

The Mane and Tail

Avoid brushing manes and tails, as even gentle brushing can cause breakage in hairs that take years to replace. The base of the mane can be brushed at the roots to stimulate growth, but any hair tangles must be separated by hand.

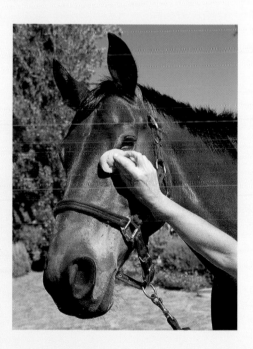

To groom the tail, take it in one hand and release a small section at a time, separating tangles and strands with the fingers of the other hand. This process can be aided by the application of a proprietary conditioning spray.

The Final Touches

Dip one sponge in warm water and wring it out, then gently wipe the horse's eyes, mouth and nostrils. With a separate sponge, wipe the dock, including the underside of the tail.

The horse's body can then be 'polished' with a folded stable rubber (rag), and the mane and tail neatened into place with a damp water brush. The final touch is the application with a brush of hoof oil on the inside and outside of the hooves, not only for appearance but to improve their condition. Once the rugs are replaced, the horse can return clean and relaxed to its stable.

Grooming for grass-kept horses has to be modified, as horses living out need to retain more of the coat's natural grease for warmth and waterproofing. The eyes, nose, feet and dock should be attended to, but grooming as such should be limited to the removal of mud with a dandy-brush or rubber currycomb.

Above: *Use a clean sponge to clean around the horse's eyes.*
Inset: *A water brush is used to clean the feet, as well as the mane and tail.*

TRIMMING
THE MANE

The stable-kept riding horse will have a neatly trimmed mane and tail.

The mane is 'pulled' to a length of approximately 10cm (4in) to facilitate general neatness and ease of plaiting for competitions. Pulling a mane basically means plucking out the longest hairs to regulate the overall length. It takes practice so as not to cause the horse too much discomfort. Manes should not be cut as this tends to make them bushy.

- To pull a mane, start at the top of the neck, take a firm hold of a few hairs and with a mane comb, push the shorter hairs up against the lie of the hair. Wrap the longer hairs around the comb and, with a swift jerk, pull them out.

- Work down the mane to create the required length. If the horse is sensitive, pull the mane in short bouts over a period of a few days to avoid soreness.

- The idea is to make the mane lie flat and over to one side. This will usually be to the right but, like human hair, horse hair parts naturally in different places, so if the mane falls over to the left, deal with it on that side. Plaiting the mane over will encourage it to lie flat.

- If the mane is very thick where the headpiece of the bridle fits, a small gap can be clipped to allow the headpiece to rest more comfortably in this area.

Above: *To pull the mane, wrap the longer hairs around the comb and give a firm tug to pull them out.*

- Before competitions and while travelling, applying a tail bandage prevents rubbing and ensures the tail is kept neat.
- A tail bandage should be applied securely but not too tightly, with uniform pressure all the way down. The fastening should also be secured with tape, and a tail guard applied over the top while travelling, to avoid the horse rubbing the fastenings loose.

THE TAIL

A well-tailored tail should be narrow at the top (the dock end), and taper to fullness, ending in a straight-cut 'bang'.

- To create this effect, the long hairs under the dock are removed either by careful pulling or trimming with clippers, to a point usually about one-half to two-thirds of the way down the dock.
- The ends of the tail are cut so that when the tail is carried while the horse is in motion, the end of the tail will be level with a point about 10cm (4in) below the hock.

Above right: *A well-groomed tail is free of tangles and ends in a straight edge.*
Above left: *The tail should be held up when it is trimmed.*

CLIPPING

Hairy heels can be trimmed carefully, cutting the excess hair with curved scissors pointed downward or with hand clippers. Long hairs from inside the ears may be trimmed flush with the outside of the ear, but the protective inner 'fur' should never be touched. While the long hairs at the back of the jaw can be trimmed, the long whiskers around the horse's muzzle are 'feeler' hairs, and it is very unfair to remove them for the sake of appearance.

Clipping is an acquired skill best undertaken by experienced handlers. The style of clip is dependent on the amount of work the horse is doing, as this determines how much it is likely to sweat. Horses in full regular work can be 'clipped out' (given a full body clip) or clipped only to the elbows and thighs. The latter, with a saddle patch left on, is known as a hunter clip. Hair left on the legs affords protection from the weather, and the saddle patch can be useful on particularly thin-skinned, cold-backed or sensitive horses. A blanket clip, where the legs and an exercise blanket shaped area over the body are left unclipped, is a good option for the horse in lighter work. A trace clip involves clipping a strip from the horse's belly to the gullet, and is often used on ponies in less regular work.

Above: *Hunter clip with legs clipped as for full clip.*

Above: *Blanket clip.*

Above: *Low trace clip.*

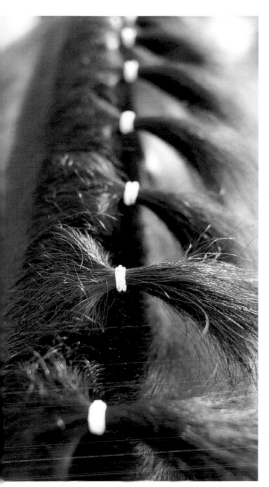

PLAITING

For shows and special events, a plaited mane is considered a sign of good turnout and of respect to judges or officials. For show classes, dressage and event dressage, you will feel out of place if you don't plait. In top-class show jumping, however, plaiting is less common as horses are often jumping late into the night and on several days a week.

Basic plaiting involves sectioning the hair in widths roughly equivalent to one mane comb, then plaiting uniformly down to the very end of the hair, and securing with a rubber band before rolling or folding the plait under neatly and finishing by securing with another rubber band, or stitching with a needle and thread. Dressage plaits are graduated in size to show off the outline of the neck, and finished with a covering of white tape.

Full tails (i.e. unpulled) can be neatly plaited to improve turnout on competition days.

Above: *Manes and tails are frequently plaited (braided) for competitions.*

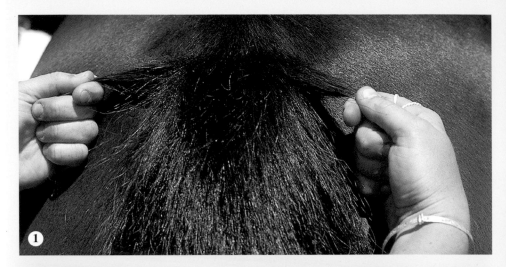

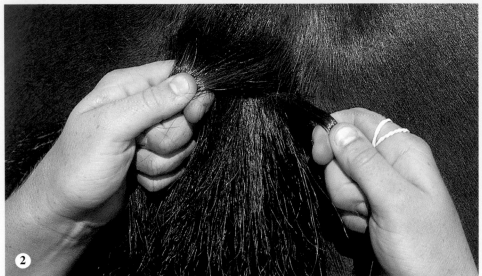

Take three small bunches of hair from either side and from the middle, then start plaiting (braiding) as for a French plait (1). Take a few more strands of hair from the sides as you work (2). Continue until almost at the base of the dock and then plait (braid) normally (3).

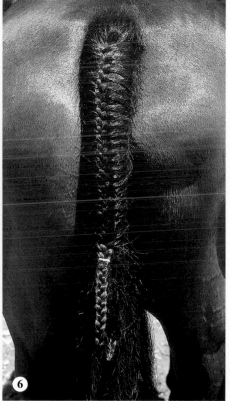

Tie up the end of the plait (braid) with a rubber band before turning the loose end under to form a neat loop (4). Use a second rubber band to secure the plait just below the dock of the tail (5 and 6).

Remember the age-old maxim 'no foot, no horse'? Feet problems will lead to lameness, and a lame horse cannot be ridden. It is therefore essential for every horse owner to understand the structure of the foot and be aware of what can go wrong.

Regular visits from a farrier are essential– even if your horse is not shod, the hooves will need to be trimmed. However, you cannot rely on your farrier alone; you will have to attend to your horse's feet, picking out the hooves at least once a day to ensure the feet remain healthy. Check for stones, as well as any injury, such as puncture wounds or bruising. In addition, check for cracking and thrush. Take immediate action if anything is wrong.

A horse's foot consists of three parts – the wall, sole and frog. The wall is horny and non-sensitive, while the frog and sole comprise both horny and sensitive parts. The interior of the foot contains sensitive, fleshy tissue as well as blood and nerves.

When the horse's foot is on the ground we see the wall, which extends from the coronet at the top of the hoof, just as a fingernail grows from the cuticle. The toe (the thickest part of the wall, at the front of the hoof), quarters (on each side) and heel (at the back) are all part of the wall. The slightly concave sole under the foot provides some protection, but it is thin and can be bruised or injured by sharp stones and hard ground. The rubbery frog,

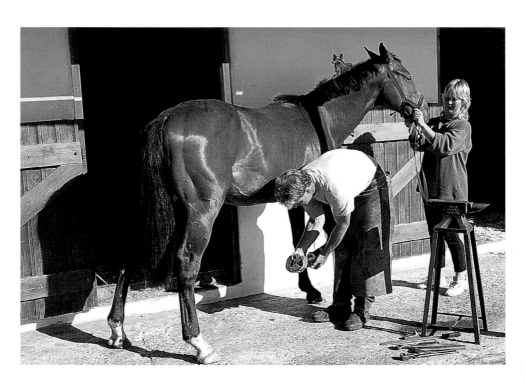

Above: *A farrier checks a horse's hooves before he begins the task of shoeing the feet.*

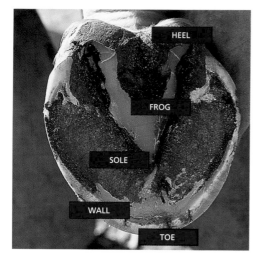

on the ground with the addition of studs. Horseshoes may also be used for medical reasons, in the case of injury or to remedy an abnormality.

- Shoes should be replaced every four to six weeks, depending on the work the horse does and the hardness of the ground he works on. You will soon learn how to assess when shoes are worn out or loose, or when the foot has grown too long.
- Check the clinches and clips regularly to ensure the shoe has not twisted.
- Use the tip of a hoof pick between the shoe and hoof to check the shoe fits snugly. If it is not loose or worn, but the horn has grown over the edges, your farrier may refit the same shoes after trimming the hooves
- If a horse throws a shoe, try to find it — particularly if he was shod recently.

which is rather like a natural shock absorber and antislip pad, has a groove or cleft down the middle, giving the horse a better foothold

When the horse moves, irrespective of speed or gait, the heel should always meet the ground first, so that it and the frog absorb most of the weight.

Hooves, like fingernails, are constantly growing; it takes approximately six months for a new hoof wall to grow. Whether or not the horse is shod, hooves need to be trimmed and rasped regularly, which also helps prevent chipping and cracking.

SHOEING

Modern farriers serve an apprenticeship of three to four years and must then pass an examination. Use a qualified farrier as bad shoeing can result in injury and disfigurement and be aware that it is illegal in some countries (such as the UK) to shoe even your own horse without a license.

Shoeing protects the foot, particularly when the horse is ridden on roads and hard ground, and it provides a means of improving the grip

There are various types of horseshoes, from thin aluminium shoes used on racehorses to heavy shoes for working heavy horses. Your farrier will advise you on the best design and weight suitable for your horse.

The traditional method of hot shoeing is still practised by skilled farriers today and involves making the shoe from raw iron and shaping it to the horse's foot while it is still hot. Traditionally, this method is preferred, but is not always practical, even though portable forges are available.

Modern shoes are machine made and simply adjusted by the farrier to fit the horse. Referred to as cold shoeing, this enables the farrier to work at the stable rather than having the horse brought to him. The shoe is nailed to the insensitive wall of the hoof with specially designed horseshoe nails. The ends that protrude through the wall are turned over and

Top: *The structure of the underside of a horse's hoof.*

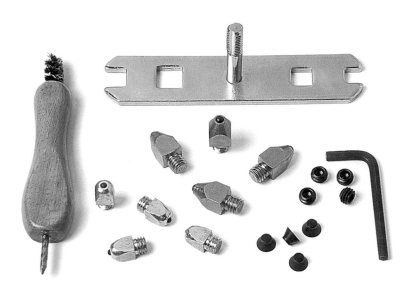

bent downwards to form a clinch, which is neatened with a rasp. Many farriers recommend using horseshoes with quarter and/or toe-clips in order to keep the shoe in place more securely.

If you are competing in cross-country competitions or riding on slippery ground, it is advisable to use studs. Your farrier will need to make holes in the shoes to accommodate the studs. He will usually ask in advance if these are required, and whether you want them in all the shoes or only the hind ones, which is the norm. He will help you decide what is best for you and your horse. Stud kits contain a variety of studs – big, small, pointed or chunky – as well as the tools required to insert and remove them. They are also available loose. Never leave studs in the shoes after working or competing, and unless the shoes are soon going to be replaced, always plug the holes with greased

cottonwool (cotton) or with sleepers to prevent dirt and sand getting in the thread.

Once the horse has been shod, the farrier will ask you to trot the horse out to ensure that he is level and not sore or lame. Run alongside the horse with a long, loose lead rein. If he is not balanced, the farrier will rectify the problem immediately.

The shoes of horses that are not being worked for more than a month may be removed so the hooves can grow naturally without interference. Usually, the farrier will remove shoes for you, unless there is an emergency and the shoe has, for instance, twisted out of place or has become dangerously loose and could harm the foot. Ask him to show you how to remove the shoe correctly. It must be eased off gently after the clinches have been straightened, or cut off. Shoes must never be ripped off not even if they are loose.

Top: *Items from a stud kit include two different types of studs, sleepers and tools used to insert and remove the studs and clean the stud holes.*

The farrier examines the horse's foot before he starts work. This young horse has never been shod before.

Now he cleans out the frog and trims any ragged parts of the sole. Then he will use a rasp to create a level bearing surface.

The foot must be clean before it can be shod. The farrier picks out all the mud and dirt from the foot using a hoof pick.

Choosing a shoe that is the correct weight, size and shape for the work the horse is to do, he nails it to the foot.

The protruding nail ends are turned over and twisted off to form clinches. The rasp is then used to neaten the edges.

When using the hot-shoeing method, the shoe is made to fit the foot. While the farrier trims and rasps the horse's hooves, the shoes are heated in a small, portable forge.

The farrier shapes the hot horseshoes on his portable anvil to ensure that they fit each of the horse's hooves.

The farrier places the red-hot shoe on the bottom of the horse's foot. The mark left by the hot metal indicates where the foot and shoe make contact, showing where he needs to alter the shape of the shoe or rasp the foot further.

Although the shoe is red-hot when it is placed on the foot, the heat does not cause the horse any pain.

OILING AND DRESSING

This is a surprisingly controversial subject. Some people recommend oiling brittle hooves daily with a proprietary brand of hoof oil, while others insist that this simply creates a greasy film that attracts dirt. Although some people prefer the old-fashioned mixture of hoof oil and Stockholm tar, by far the most common and sensible approach is to use proprietary hoof dressings, applied according to the manufacturer's instructions. Hoof oils and dressings are painted onto the wall of the hoof. Stockholm tar, used successfully to treat thrush and other diseases and to keep the hoof dry, should be applied to the sole of the foot, particularly in the cleft of the frog.

A good rule is to keep the hoof dry when conditions are wet and prevent it from drying out when the weather is hot.

Above: *It is essential to trot a horse out after it has been shod to ensure that it is balanced and sound.*

TACK AND EQUIPMENT

If you have been riding at a school, or even leasing a horse or pony, you may already have some tack and riding equipment – perhaps even blankets and a basic grooming kit. If not, you will have to start from scratch.

While the tack required is determined by the type of horse you have, as well as the kind of riding you will be doing, additional articles such as rugs and blankets which fall under the heading of horse clothing, and so on are all affected more by the home you have arranged for him and the climate in which you live.

In addition to all the riding paraphernalia, you should equip yourself with a good first-aid kit (see p171), a selection of items required for travelling (i.e. for transporting your horse, see pp70–73), and other items needed to keep your horse well groomed and healthy. Go into any tack or saddlery shop and you will realize that there is a vast array of equipment and clothing available for both horse and rider: rows of different saddles and fittings; all kinds of bridles, halters and reins; bits made for different purposes from metal, rubber or synthetic materials; numnahs or saddle pads of varying shapes, sizes and colours; piles of blankets, rugs and day sheets.

Boots, bandages and leg-wraps also come in a variety of shapes and sizes, made from a range of materials. There are brushes, combs, hoof picks, rubber bands and blunt needles for plaiting; different oils for maintaining hooves or various oils available for leatherware; soaps and shampoo for cleaning tack; and additional soaps and shampoos for cleaning horses. However, there is no need to buy it all. Start with the essentials and then, if necessary, add to your equipment as you can afford it.

Left: *Regular cleaning and maintenance not only protects valuable tack, but also enables the rider to spot potential problems before they occur.*
Inset: *Experienced riders use the double bridle to allow the application of light, almost invisible aids.*

▸ SADDLES AND THE RIDER'S SEAT ◂

There are two primary types of 'seat' (or posture): the basic, or dressage, seat used for general riding, and the light, or forward, seat used for riding across country and jumping. Whatever the type, the correct seat is not just aesthetically pleasing, but essential for effective communication with the horse. The aids can only be applied properly if the rider is sitting securely, in balance, and with the suppleness needed to go with the horse's movement rather than stiffening against it. The three main styles of saddle are general purpose, jumping and dressage.

THE BASIC, OR DRESSAGE, SEAT

The most commonly used seat for all riding on the flat is the basic, or dressage, seat. You can use the basic seat with either a general-purpose or a dressage saddle, but in a specially designed dressage saddle the depth of seat and length of leg will be greater.

In the basic seat the rider sits upright and a theoretical line can be drawn through the rider's shoulder, hip and heel. Other elements of the basic seat can vary as not all riders – or horses – are the same shape and size, but this line is constant.

PARTS OF THE SADDLE

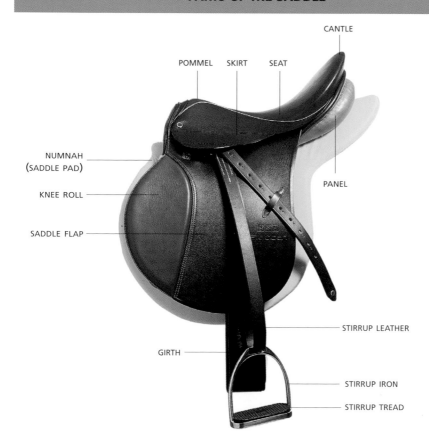

CANTLE

POMMEL   SKIRT   SEAT

NUMNAH
(SADDLE PAD)

KNEE ROLL

SADDLE FLAP

PANEL

STIRRUP LEATHER

GIRTH

STIRRUP IRON

STIRRUP TREAD

Good horses and good riders come in all shapes and sizes, so if you have ever been told that to look elegant on a horse you have to be tall, slim and long-legged, forget it. Granted, longer arms and a short lower back will make it easier for a rider to carry the hands low and stable, while a round inner thigh will be less easy to rest flat against the saddle than a slim one, but every individual, with training and development, can make the most of their own shape to become an effective and elegant rider.

In a good dressage, or basic, seat the buttocks should be in the lowest part of the saddle and the rider's body weight should be distributed equally over both seat bones and thighs, with the muscles free of tension. Any tightness will raise the seat, which will result in the rider sitting 'above' the horse.

The upper body should be 'tall in the saddle', with relaxed shoulders – poised but not tense – with the head proud and looking forward. The upper arms and elbows are carried close to the body and the lower arms low towards the horse's withers. The hands are held with thumbs uppermost, closed but not tightened over the reins. Clamped elbows will lead to stiffness in the hands, while sticking-out elbows destabilize the upper body, arms and hands. From the side, the bit, rein, and hand-to-elbow line should be straight and unbroken, as any break will affect the rider's ability to maintain a soft contact with the horse's mouth and apply sensitive rein aids.

In later lessons, further development of this toned poise allows the rider to use the back muscles as a refined aid in the half-halt and in transitions. The phrase 'bracing the back' really means more of a 'hold-then-flex' reaction than an actual bracing.

The knee is bent so that the lower leg slopes backward and the calf rests in contact with the horse. The foot is slightly behind the girth and under the rider's centre of gravity (the hip-heel angle), and the thigh should rest flat against the saddle. Turning the knee or thigh out causes tension and destabilizes the seat.

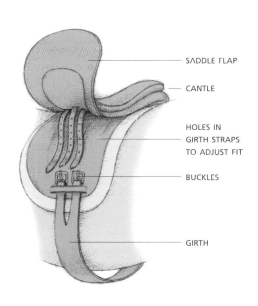

SADDLE FLAP

CANTLE

HOLES IN
GIRTH STRAPS
TO ADJUST FIT

BUCKLES

GIRTH

Inset: *The traditional dressage saddle has long flaps to accommodate the rider's length of leg.*

too short will lead to a 'chair seat', in which case the rider will not be able to sit deep in the saddle and his lower leg will be stiff and too far forwards. The ball of the foot, resting on the stirrup, allows the ankle to flex and the heel to lower slightly. 'Heels down' is often heard in lessons, but it does not mean with exaggerated pressure. With the leg in the correct position, the knee and ankle absorb the horse's motion. The toes should face forward, not be turned too far in or out.

In conventional riding, it is important not to ride with stirrups that hang too long, as this reduces the movement-absorbing capacity of the knee and causes a lack of balance. The rider will end up sitting on his fork rather than his seat bones, and will not be able to control his lower leg. Conversely, stirrups that are

THE LIGHT, OR JUMPING, SEAT

For riding over fences, hacking (riding) out, or when schooling young horses, the rider needs, in degrees, to be able to take more weight off the horse's back and adjust quickly and smoothly to changes in balance and pace. A jumping saddle or a general-purpose saddle with a shorter stirrup length allows for a more forward position of the knee. For a hack round the field after a schooling session, for example, the stirrups would be raised by just one or two holes. For a jumping or cross-country session, the rider may raise his or her stirrups between four to six holes. The shortest stirrup length is generally used for the fastest work, such as the steeplechase phase in a three-day event, when the rider's weight needs to be completely off the horse's back.

Above: *A simple pad saddle is ideal for a pony.*
Inset: *The jumping saddle helps the rider to go with the horse's forward movement over the jump. The knee rolls support the rider in the lighter seat.*
Top: *Girths are made from various materials, such as (from left to right) synthetic, padded, elasticated, wicking and leather (for a dressage saddle).*

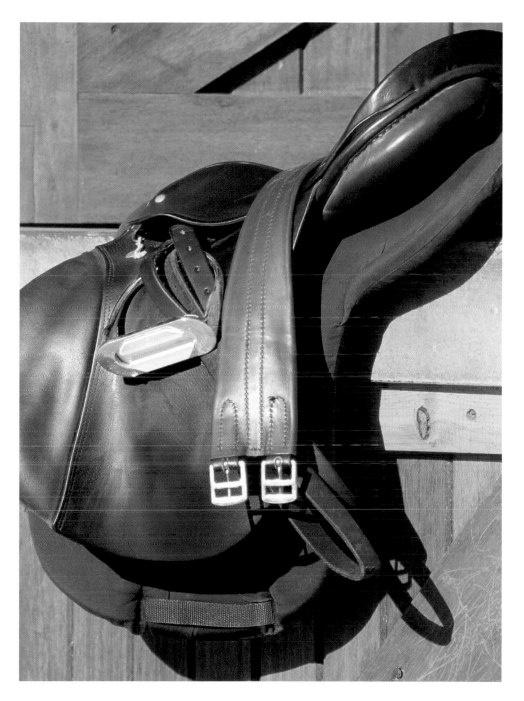

Above: *A well-made, professionally fitted saddle will improve comfort for both horse and rider.*

This is done from the horse's left, or 'near' side. If using a numnah, or saddle pad, place this on the horse's back first, a little further up on the withers than it will eventually rest.

- With the stirrup irons run up and the girth (attached on the right side) placed ready over the top of the saddle, lift the saddle clear of the horse (1)
- Allow it to settle gently on its back, then slide both the saddle and pad into position (2). Check that the pad is flat, unwrinkled and evenly positioned on both sides before taking the girth down on the right.

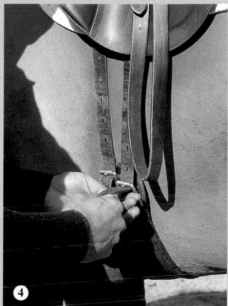

- Return to the left side of the horse and fasten the girth securely enough to keep the saddle in place (3 and 4).
- When the saddle is correctly placed, the girth should lie flat about 10cm (4in) from the point of the elbow.
- The girth can be tightened later by degrees before mounting, but it is not fair on a horse to immediately fasten its girth up to the riding position. This can cause discomfort and abrasion and can also make the horse girth-shy.

HEAD COLLARS AND HALTERS

Head collars (headstalls), sometimes called halters, are usually the first pieces of equipment a horse will encounter. These are made of leather or synthetic fabric, which is easier to keep clean. They usually consist of a headpiece, noseband, cheekpieces and throat latch buckled or stitched together. The head collar (headstall) is slid over the horse's nose and under the throat before being fastened over his neck, behind the ears. A simple halter is made of webbing or rope and slides over the nose and behind the ears. All types are used with a lead-rein or rope, enabling you to tie the horse up if you have to, or to lead it.

BRIDLES AND BITS

Bridles are available in various styles and shapes and should be chosen for the job the horse is to do. In competitions, rules usually specify which bits and bridles may be used, so check the rule books if you compete. Generally, the simplest option that works for horse and rider is the best.

THE SNAFFLE BRIDLE

Most riders should start off with a simple snaffle bridle. The primary difference between the types of snaffle bridle is in the choice of noseband. The purpose of the noseband is to keep the horse's top and bottom jaws aligned.

Above left: *Head collar (headstall).*
Above right: *Flash noseband.*

DIFFERENT TYPES OF NOSEBAND

- The **standard cavesson noseband** is the simplest noseband, and this fits around the nose above the bit.
- The **flash noseband** is a type of cavesson, but it is fitted with an additional narrow strap, which in turn is attached to the front of the noseband below the bit. It is often used in basic training, generally to help settle horses in the mouth.
- **Drop nosebands** are fastened below the bit and are useful for stronger horses, preventing them from opening their mouths and evading the bit. The nosepiece should rest on the bony part of the nose and should not restrict the horse's breathing.
- **Grakle nosebands** consist of two straps that cross the front of the nose over a small padded leather disc. Their action is similar to a flash noseband, and they sit well clear of the nostrils. They are most popular with event riders who find them useful for controlling their horses during the cross-country phase.
- The **kineton noseband**, used with a snaffle bit, can be useful for horses that pull excessively, but this should only be used by experienced riders. The action on the nose keeps the bit forward, thus reducing the pressure the bit would normally have on the mouth.

NOTE: The cavesson is the only noseband that should be used with a pelham bit or double bridle, while only a cavesson or flash noseband may be attached to a standing martingale, which incorporates straps to keep the horse's head down.

Top left: *Drop noseband.*
Top right: *Grakle noseband.*

THE DOUBLE BRIDLE

A double bridle incorporates two bits, a bridoon (which is a form of snaffle) and a curb bit (weymouth), each of which acts in a different way. Commonly used by experienced riders in advanced dressage competitions, on reasonably advanced-level horses, the double bridle allows more refined use of the aids and a more definitive action on the jaw, but should only be introduced once the horse accepts the bit confidently and happily. It should not be used by novice riders or on novice horses.

THE HACKAMORE BRIDLE

This is a bitless bridle that has a poll action and also acts on the nose and chin-groove. These parts of the horse are all sensitive even if there is no bit. If used incorrectly, especially by an inexperienced rider, a hackamore can be damaging and may cause serious injury.

Reins are made of leather and may be plain, laced or plaited. Some combine rubber with leather for a better grip. Two reins are attached, one to each side of the bit, and buckled together.

PARTS OF THE SNAFFLE BRIDLE

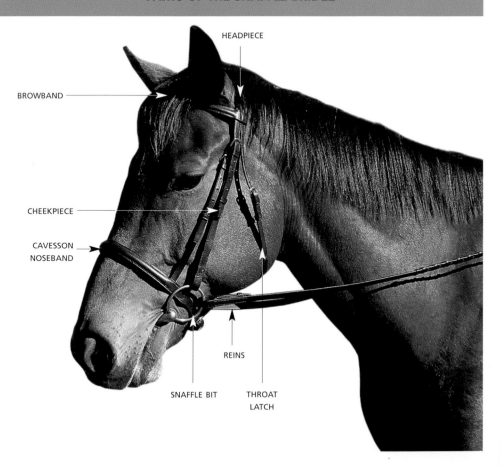

HEADPIECE

BROWBAND

CHEEKPIECE

CAVESSON NOSEBAND

REINS

SNAFFLE BIT

THROAT LATCH

BITS

Bits are made of stainless steel or compound metals, as well as synthetics, rubber or vulcanite. Together with related parts of the bridle, different bits act on various parts of the mouth, as well as the nose, chin-groove and poll (top of the head). To be effective, the bit must fit properly and be used correctly. A thin bit is generally more severe than a thicker one.

A **snaffle bit** is the most commonly used bit. There are several different types, the most common being the plain, jointed snaffle. A single-jointed loose-ring snaffle has a mild but effective action, primarily on the lips and corners of the mouth. The eggbutt snaffle, which has smooth, unhinged joints at the sides, has a similar action and gives good results in horses with sensitive mouths. D-ring snaffles, with side rings shaped like a D rather than being round, also have a single joint in the centre, but the metal, except for the joint itself, is sometimes rubber covered. A cheek snaffle or fulmer has bars on either side, which can be useful when a horse is disobedient or difficult to turn. Side pieces may be jointed or fixed.

Some snaffles have a double joint, including the French snaffle, the KK (a popular German bit) and the Doctor Bristol, which has a rectangular central plate with squared sides that can be set at an angle to press on the tongue. As the Doctor Bristol's action is quite harsh, it is not permitted for dressage, but can be useful for experienced cross-country riders on strong horses.

Twisted snaffles, including fulmers with twisted mouth elements, are very severe and not recommended. Various gags, including gag snaffles, use a pulley effect to raise the head and are sometimes used to control difficult or strong horses. These bits have a poll action, that is, they work on the top of the head, as well as on the lips, corners of the mouth and the tongue. They are severe, so should be employed with caution.

In addition to jointed snaffles, several straight-bar types are made from steel, tough vulcanite, rubber and various other synthetic materials. Note that some horses learn to draw their tongues away from a straight-bar snaffle bit, or push their tongues over it, negating the action of the bit.

The **pelham** is a curb bit that has a straight, curved or jointed bar with a curb-chain and may be used with single or double reins, but only with a cavesson noseband. The top rein, which is attached to the rings above the bar, acts on the mouth and tongue of the horse, while the bottom rein, fitted to larger rings below the bar, acts on the chin-groove and poll. When used with only one pair of reins, leather couplings (rein connectors) are fitted between each pair of rings. The Kimblewick is a single-rein pelham, with a straight bar and small tongue-groove.

Top: *The hackamore bridle controls the horse by means of pressure on its neck.*

TYPES OF BITS

DOUBLE-JOINTED LOOSE-RING SNAFFLE

DOUBLE-JOINTED EGGBUTT SNAFFLE

FRENCH-LINK SNAFFLE

SINGLE-JOINTED LOOSE-RING SNAFFLE

SINGLE-JOINTED EGGBUTT (D-RING) SNAFFLE

RUBBER-COVERED D-RING SNAFFLE

DOCTOR BRISTOL

DOUBLE-JOINTED SNAFFLE WITH CHEEKS (DICK CHRISTIAN)

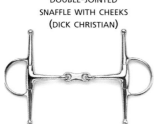

PELHAM WITH RUBBER MOUTHPIECE WITH CURB CHAIN

EGGBUTT BRIDOON WITH CURB BIT AND CURB CHAIN FOR A DOUBLE BRIDLE

ROPE GAG

DUTCH GAG

AMERICAN GAG

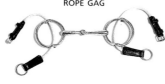

LOOSE-RING PLASTIC SNAFFLE

HACKAMORE

KIMBLEWICK (SINGLE-REIN PELHAM)

STRAIGHT-BAR RUBBER SNAFFLE

PORTUGUESE GAG

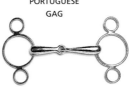

AUXILIARY EQUIPMENT

Auxiliary reins and martingales are used for training and lunging horses.

A simple lunging cavesson is designed to be used with a lunge-rein, which is usually attached to the central ring (one of three) on the noseband. It is made with broader leather than a regular bridle and it has a well-padded noseband. When in use, the jowl-strap is buckled firmly round the horse's nose so that the cheekpieces do not pull forward during work.

Side-reins and running reins are also used when lunging. When correctly adjusted, they encourage the horse to lower his head and neck and soften his back.

Martingales, used to gain extra control of the horse and stop him from raising and throwing his head, are also made of leather. Incorporating neck straps to keep them in place, martingales are looped over the girth and taken between the forelegs before being connected to the bridle or reins. A standing martingale is attached to the cavesson noseband (or cavesson section of a flash noseband), while a running martingale – which gives more freedom of movement – is connected to the reins by means of rings, allowing it to run freely up and down the reins, which should be fitted with rubber martingale-stops. An Irish martingale keeps the reins in place and stops them going over the horse's head.

Breastplates made of leather or webbing, sometimes with additional strapping, are attached to the front of the saddle on each side of the horse's neck and to the girth to prevent the saddle from slipping backwards. They are used by both event riders and show jumpers.

Top: *Martingales (left) and breastplates (right) are both useful auxiliary items of tack.*

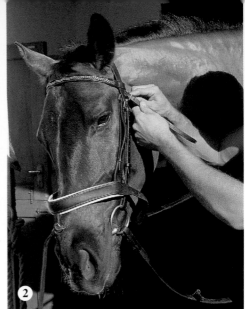

PUTTING ON THE BRIDLE

- To put on the bridle, which should be correctly adjusted beforehand, approach the horse from the left (or near) side and carefully place the reins over its head. Holding the bridle midway, remove the head collar (headstall), placing your right hand over the horse's nose and taking the bridle into your right hand.
- With your left hand, position the bit under the horse's mouth (1).
- Exerting a light pressure on the corners of the horse's mouth will encourage the horse to open its mouth and accept the bit. As the bit goes in, with you taking care not to bang the horse's teeth, you can reach up and place the headpiece over one ear at a time.
- After checking that no mane or forelock is caught in the leather work, and the bridle is lying comfortably and without twisting, you can fasten the throatlatch (2) (allow one hand's width between it and the horse's throat), and then the noseband (3).

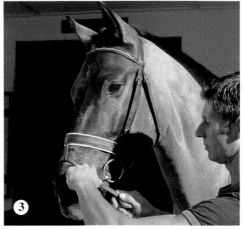

- A cavesson noseband should lie one finger's width below the bottom of the horse's cheekbone and should be fastened to allow one finger's width between the noseband and the horse's nasal bone. A drop noseband should lie four fingers' width above the horse's nostrils and should be fastened securely enough to prevent the horse from crossing his jaw, but with enough room for the horse to be able to mouth the bit comfortably.

LEGS: BOOTS

Brushing boots are used on all four legs to protect them both in work or while turned out in the field. They are commonly made of easy-care synthetic material, with Velcro fastenings and extra padding on the inside. Specialized boots, with a higher degree of protection, can be used for cross-country.

- **Fetlock boots** cover the fetlock joints of the hind legs and are commonly used in show-jumping events.
- **Tendon boots** afford protection to the vulnerable tendon area. Those open at the front are used on the forelegs in show jumping.
- **Overreach boots** (bell boots) give protection to the coronary area and the bulbs of the heels, especially when jumping or lungeing. Usually made from rubber, they are either pulled on over the front hooves or fastened with Velcro. These are often used when travelling.
- **Coronet boots** fulfill a similar purpose to overreach boots but fit a little higher over the lower part of the fetlock.
- **Travelling boots** (shipping boots) are long, thickly padded leggings that protect from the hock or knee area right down over the coronary band. Travelling boots should fit snugly, but should not be too tight or exert pressure, and all fastenings should be closed on the outside of the leg with the strap ends tucked away neatly and facing the back.

LEG PROTECTION

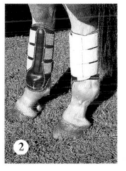

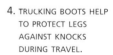

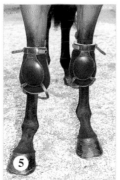

1. LEATHER BRUSHING BOOTS WITH STRAPS AND BUCKLES.

2. COLOURFUL BRUSHING BOOTS SECURED WITH VELCRO.

3. TENDON BOOTS HAVE A PROTECTIVE PAD DOWN THE BACK.

4. TRUCKING BOOTS HELP TO PROTECT LEGS AGAINST KNOCKS DURING TRAVEL.

5. KNEE CAPS ARE USED TO PROTECT THE KNEES DURING TRAVEL.

6. A RUBBER RING IS USED IF A HORSE BRUSHES ON THE CORONET.

BANDAGES

Bandages (called wraps or polo wraps in the USA), are used for protection during work – most often for dressage training and during cross-country. They are normally made of wool or a cotton mix, with varying degrees of elasticity, and are usually fitted over a layer of soft wadding (padding) or a purpose-made bandage liner. Bandages must always be applied evenly and with the correct tension to avoid impeding the blood supply to

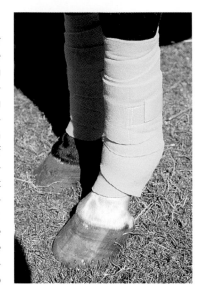

the legs or causing a pressure injury, so the less experienced horse owner may find boots a safer option. Travelling bandages are made of wider, thicker material. These bandages are applied over a thick layer of padding and secured by adhesive tape.

When bandages are used over shock-absorbing material for cross-country, the Velcro or tie fastenings should also be taped for extra security.

Above: *Stable bandages may be used in the event of injury to provide extra warmth when travelling.*

RUGS AND BLANKETS

In colder climates, horses in work are clipped when they develop their thick winter coats, then rugged-up (blanketed) at night and during periods of inactivity. This is done because a horse that has sweated under a thick coat could experience difficulties with drying off in cold wet weather, and is then at risk of catching a chill.

In the stable, the horse should not be excessively rugged-up (blanketed) as this can make it more susceptible to chills. Some horses feel the cold more than others, so much of the philosophy of rugging-up relies on common sense.

With the number of styles readily available, the well-dressed horse could be in possession of an entire wardrobe of rugs (blankets), but most owners will manage with just two or three.

• The **quilted stable rug** in various weights has generally replaced a night or day rug over blankets. Not only are modern stable rugs easier to maintain but they are lighter on the horse's back and, when secured with cross straps under the horse's stomach, do not normally need a surcingle or roller to keep them in place (other than for

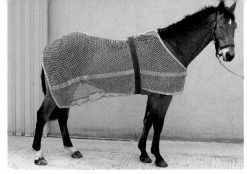

SWEAT BLANKET

FLY (OR DAY) SHEET AND MATCHING FLY FRINGE

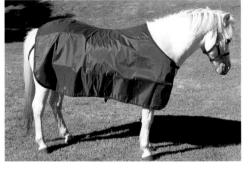

LIGHT, UNLINED BUT WATERPROOF RAIN SHEET

NEW ZEALAND-TYPE RUG

additional stability), so there are no pressure points on the horse's back.

- **Turn-out rugs,** all-weather rugs used in the field or paddock, not only help to keep horses mud-free and dry, but also enable the clipped horse to go out in colder weather. Turn-out rugs can be made from weatherproofed lined nylon or lined canvas. A popular version is generally known as a New Zealand rug.
- **Day rugs** are made of wool blanketing and are most commonly used at competitions to keep the horse warm during waiting periods. They are often made in the owner's or sponsor's colours.

- **Sweat rugs** (or sweat sheets, or coolers), are made in absorbent fabric and used in the same way as day rugs, as well as for cooling down after exercise or while travelling.
- **Summer sheets,** made from cotton or other light fabric, can be used under rugs, or while travelling in warmer times of the year, to keep the horse clean without providing warmth.
- **Exercise rugs** generally fit under the saddle and keep the horse's back and loins warm during light exercise and riding out. They are made of blanketing or weatherproof material.

RUGGING UP

Although modern lightweight rugs make rugging up (blanketing) easier than in the past, if it is not done properly, a flapping rug can easily startle a horse.

The best way to put on a rug (blanket) is to fold it in two, from front to back, with the lining uppermost, and place it over the horse, setting it higher on the withers than it will eventually rest (1). Fold the back portion down over the horse (2). After checking that the rug is evenly placed and free of wrinkles (3), fasten the cross straps or surcingle (roller), before fastening the rug at the front (4).

Your horse should be tied up or in the stable with the door closed during this process, as in the event of a horse going walkabout it is

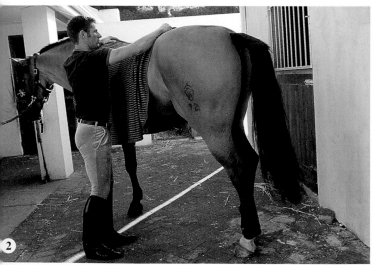

dangerous to only have a fastened front strap; the rug could slip and make the horse panic, causing an accident.

Rollers and surcingles are sometimes used over a pad placed across the back just behind the withers. They should be secure enough to keep the rug in place but not so tight as to cause the horse discomfort or force it to hold its breath all night.

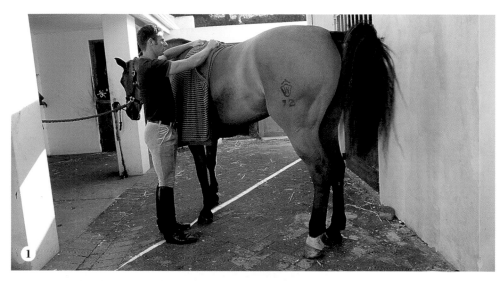

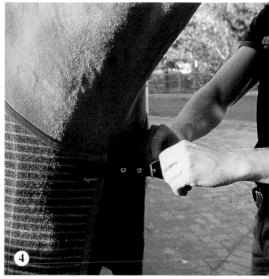

Below. *Cotton day sheets are used in countries with hot climates in order to protect horses from the sun.*

HANDLING YOUR HORSE

Horses are physically strong and must therefore be handled correctly. If you are an inexperienced rider, always buy a horse that has been broken in, is familiar with humans and used to being ridden. Be aware, though, that the horse may have had earlier bad experiences you do not know about, which could result in problematic behaviour. Although horses are rarely aggressive, they can be easily frightened. Sudden movements and loud noises can spook the best-behaved animal and cause it to panic. Faced with a memory of danger, it may also react unpredictably.

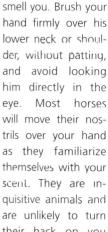

Remember that the inherent instinct of any horse is flight: rather than stay and fight, he will flee as far from danger as quickly as possible. As a result, you should learn all you can about horses' behaviour and take every safety precaution when dealing with them. They are gregarious animals and thrive on being with their own kind. They are also creatures of habit. If your horse has a set routine and at least one stable-mate, along with food, warmth and lots of love, he will be easier to handle.

Always approach and move around horses confidently, slowly and quietly. Speak firmly and kindly and never shout or behave in an aggressive manner, however frustrated or angry you may be. Kindness and patience will help develop your horse's good qualities; insensitive handling achieves the opposite.

When entering the stable, use your voice to let the horse know you are there and hold your hand out to give him the opportunity to smell you. Brush your hand firmly over his lower neck or shoulder, without patting, and avoid looking him directly in the eye. Most horses will move their nostrils over your hand as they familiarize themselves with your scent. They are inquisitive animals and are unlikely to turn their back on you unless they are fearful or angry for some reason. If they do, be sure to get out of the way as a swift kick may follow.

When approaching the horse in the paddock, move from the front towards his shoulder at the side and speak before touching him, just as you would in the stable. Generally, you should not stand directly in front of or directly behind a horse, especially if you are not familiar with its behaviour.

Left: *A group of riders and their horses enjoy the shared experience of a leisurely outride on a cold and misty winter's morning.*
Inset: *Riding school pupils benefit from professional instruction and well-schooled horses.*

▸ MOUNTING AND DISMOUNTING ◂

The standard way of mounting and dismounting a horse should be adhered to, simply because it is the safest way. A well-trained horse should always stand obediently for its rider to get on and off.

When pulling down or adjusting the stirrups or tightening the girth – which should always be checked before mounting – keep hold of the horse, even when the reins are over its head, by putting an arm through the reins. Loose horses can be dangerous to themselves and others.

Your instructor – who should be a trained rider and teacher – will advise on stirrup length, but generally, if you stretch your arm out along the stirrup, the correct length for you will be the approximate distance from your armpit to your fist.

WHEN MOUNTING:

- Stand on the left side of the horse with your back to its head. Hold the reins in your left hand with slightly more contact on the right rein in case the horse starts to move, and place your left hand on the base of the horse's neck. Turn the outside of the stirrup iron towards you with your right hand (1).
- As you place the ball of your left foot in the stirrup, lean your knee towards the horse so that your toe does not dig into its side.

MOUNTING

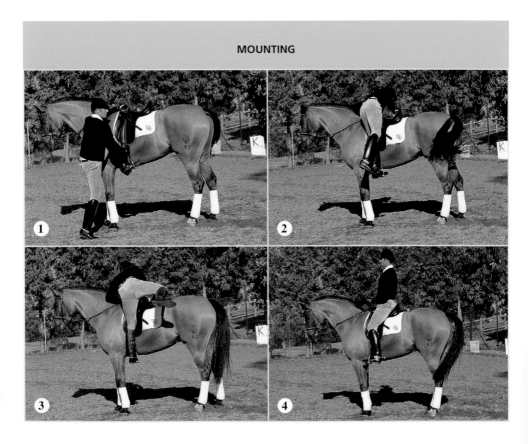

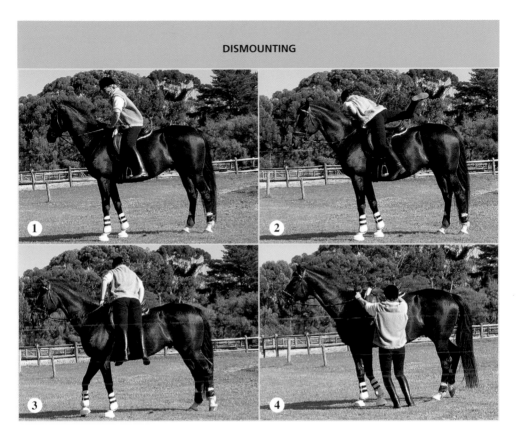

- Grasp the back of the saddle with your right hand, then hop up into the saddle by pushing up from your right foot (2).
- Swing your right leg carefully over the horse's back, taking care not to kick it (3).
- As you land softly in the saddle, put your right foot in the stirrup and take up the reins in both hands (4).

This should be one smooth movement, which takes practice. However, never think of it as cheating to use a mounting block, or to ask someone else to give you a leg-up. It is easier on both your own and the horse's back as well as the saddle.

The normal way to hold the reins is so that they run up between the third and fourth finger of each hand and out between the thumb and index finger, with the thumb on top.

WHEN DISMOUNTING:

- Rest the left hand, holding the reins, on the horse's neck (1).
- Put your right hand on the front of the saddle (the pommel), take your feet out of the stirrups and swing your right leg carefully over the back of the horse (2).
- As you do this, your body should turn towards the saddle as you slide gently to the ground (3) and (4).

It may sound like a major gymnastic exercise, but it is easy, and with a bit of practice will soon become second nature.

Ideally, your first lesson should be on the lunge. The instructor, on foot, has the horse on a long lead, called a 'lunge line', and controls the horse, which is moving in a large circle around him/her, by means of voice commands and a guiding lunge whip. Lunging allows the novice rider to concentrate on developing a relaxed position without having to worry about steering or controlling the horse. Establishing a secure seat and developing balance on the lunge will enable more rapid progress to be made later on. Once security has been established at walk, trot and canter, and you can apply the signals (aids) that control and direct the horse; joining a group of riders of a similar standard is the next progression. One-on-one lessons are not the best policy for a beginner. Instead, in a class situation, under your instructor's direction and mounted on your schoolmaster (an experienced horse used for training starter riders), you will begin thinking of yourself and developing a feeling for riding and controlling a horse.

SIGNALLING A HORSE

The signals by which we control and direct horses are known collectively as the 'aids'. The rider influences the horse through his or her seat (or weight), and leg and rein aids. In essence, weight and leg aids are forward-driving aids, while rein aids are restraining ones, but refined riding is a combination of influences, and none is ever used in isolation. Ideally, all aids should be applied lightly and reacted to immediately. There are two main points to remember. Firstly, an aid can only be responded to if the horse understands what you want Secondly, if you have to ask a bit more strongly, it should be followed up with a lighter application when you get the right response so as to maintain and improve the horse's sensitivity.

LEG AIDS
- Leg aids can be used in three ways: to drive the horse forward, to push it sideways, and to regulate its pace and movements.
- To send the horse forward, the leg is applied just behind the girth as a nudging action with the lower leg. Once the aid has been responded to, the rider's leg should hang

Above: *Leg aids are used to drive the horse forward, sideways and to regulate pace. Maintain the proper position by keeping the lower leg in light contact with the horse's side.*

relaxed at the horse's side, retaining contact as the rider's shape fits around that of the horse.

- To push the horse sideways, the outside leg (the rider's leg away from which the horse moves) is taken back slightly more behind the girth and kept in position with a nudging aid as the horse moves sideways. In moving sideways (lateral work), and on all turns and circles, the inside leg, in the relaxed position, is the regulator, creating the degree of bend and maintaining the impulsion (forward energy).

REIN AIDS

- Rein aids are given in coordination with leg and seat aids. Rein aids can be regulating, asking or allowing. The latter two are applied in tandem. For example, if an asking, restraining aid is applied in order to slow the horse, when the horse has responded the rider must also respond by yielding (or allowing) the horse to move forward in the new pace straight afterwards.

- An asking, restraining aid is applied by the rider closing the fingers on the reins while the seat and back, instead of following the movement, goes into a slight bracing action. If the horse does not respond immediately, the restrain and allow action should be reapplied until it does. Pulling continuously on the reins has an entirely negative effect; the horse will brace against the rider's hands by becoming stronger on the bit, and stiffening in the neck.

- An asking, allowing aid is used to guide the horse into a new direction, either on the straight or laterally. The rider indicates the new direction by opening the inside rein, while regulating the degree of bend or turn with the outside hand. Once the horse is established in the new direction, the rider

should have more definite contact on the outside, regulating rein, than on the inside rein. Pulling on the inside rein into a turn is negative as it disconnects the horse, producing bend in the neck alone, and the rider loses control of the horse's hindquarters.

Right (top to bottom): *The reins should run between the third and fourth finger of each hand and out between the thumb and index finger, with the thumb on top.*

- When asking the horse to change its outline (frame), such as lowering its head and neck into the relaxation position before or after work or in extended paces, the rider has to be ready to allow with the hands. In walk, for example, where the horse uses its head and neck more substantially than in the other paces, the rider's hands must allow forward movement to avoid blocking the horse's natural desire to go forward.

WEIGHT AIDS

- Weight (or seat) aids are applied by either increasing or lightening the weight on one, or both, seat bones. They can only be applied correctly when the rider can sit, in balance, through every movement of the horse without relying on the reins for balance.
- In downward transitions and with more advanced aids such as half-halts (asking the horse to change pace down), the rider's weight should have a slight bracing effect. In upward transitions (asking the horse to change pace up), the lightening of the seat encourages the forward urge, and the horse will respond by moving faster.
- In lateral work the rider's weight distribution, while still always central, will allow the horse's hind leg to step further under. In half-pass, for example, the rider will sit with slightly more weight on the inside seat bone, in the direction of the movement, to allow the outside, propelling hind leg to step more clearly under the horse.

'FEEL'

- Feel is a word often bandied around in riding circles. 'Oh, he's got such good feel' may be the comment on a particular rider, or the derogatory reverse may apply. It is not unusual for less-trained riders to experience some frustration at their real or perceived lack of this seemingly intangible talent or attribute.
- This 'feel' is an essential component of a harmonious and confident relationship between a horse and rider. If it doesn't come easily to you, it is a fallacy to think you can never achieve it – with practice you can.
- Feel is really the ability to judge the cause and effect of the horse's reaction to the rider. Examples are being able to give as the horse responds; being able to spot potential problems and deal with them before they become an issue; and being able to tell whether a horse is simply being disobedient or is just nervous. A lot of this comes with experience, but it has to be the right kind of experience.
- A well-trained horse is the best professor of feel as it will teach a rider, literally, how good it feels when he or she gets it right. A good instructor will always communicate the idea to his pupil by asking, 'How did that feel?' The novice rider has to go through something of a learning curve of trial and error to find out what it takes to make it feel right and how to achieve it consistently in the future.
- The ideal feel: If you look at a very good horse and rider combination at work in dressage, jumping or cross-country, it almost seems as if the rider is doing nothing, while the horse looks balanced, performs with brilliance and is in complete harmony with its rider. It takes a combination of attributes, one of that is good training of both halves of the combination, to achieve this 'state of grace'. Feel in a rider can be described as a mix of concentration, quick reaction, sensitivity, adaptability and a feeling for rhythm and movement, with the added ingredient of a relaxed and sympathetic attitude.

CONTACT

- This is a big part of the feel and coordination that makes the aids work smoothly and effectively. The rider has to develop the ability to always allow the horse relaxation in its head, neck and mouth, while maintaining contact with the bit.

- There are three basic rein positions. When the horse is 'on a contact' or 'on the bit', there is a consistent, soft connection from the horse's mouth to the rider's hands at all times and the horse is happy to accept the rein aids without resistance. When the horse is 'on long rein', its head and neck are carried in the natural rather than rounded position, while the rider retains a soft allowing contact. When the horse is on a 'loose rein', the rider has given the reins away completely, holding them on the buckle rather than on a contact.

Riding is really the art of communication between a willing horse and a sympathetic rider. Finesse, skill, training and coordination result in perfect partnership and harmony. Ideal examples are dressage rider Nicole Uphoff of Germany and Rembrandt, show jumper Rodrigo Pessoa of Brazil and Gandini Baloubet du Rouet, or three-day eventer Blyth Tait of New Zealand and Chesterfield. Their level of horsemanship may seem unattainable, but that is the fascination of learning to ride. It is a process that never comes to an end.

RIDING AIDS
AND CORRECT SEAT

The rider should look straight ahead, with the head high and the chin up.

Sit 'tall in the saddle', with a straight back, but without any tension in the upper body.

The elbows should be bent and a straight line maintained from the bit through the reins to the forearm.

The seat should rest in the lower part of the saddle, with the weight evenly distributed on both seat bones.

The knees are bent slightly and relaxed, and should not be used to grip the saddle.

The lower leg should slope backward from the knee, with the calf in contact with the horse's side.

The ball of the foot, resting on the stirrup, should be under the rider's centre of gravity.

WALK

The walk is a four-time (beat) gait, with each leg moving individually and a clear one-two-three-four beat being heard. In walk the rider maintains the basic seat, keeping a straight line between the shoulder, hip and heel. the lower back and hips and forearms are relaxed and able to move with the horse's natural rhythm. The horse uses its head and neck more significantly during each walk stride than in the other paces. If the rider prevents this, it can spoil the rhythm. This rider could allow a little more with her hands.

TROT

The trot is a two-time (beat) pace, with the horse's legs moving in diagonal pairs. In a rising trot, the rider sits and rises in time (beat) to the up and down movement. In a sitting trot, the rider must allow his or her body to absorb the movement, sitting deep in the saddle in the classic position. This horse is a little behind the vertical in its head carriage. Some more forward strides ridden in rising trot with lowered hands will refresh the quality of both the trot pace and the horse's outline as it is allowed to stretch its neck more.

CANTER

This is a three-time (beat) pace with the horse's legs moving in the sequence: outside hind, inside hind and outside fore, inside fore, followed by a moment of suspension, when all four legs are off the ground, before the sequence repeats itself. The rider should maintain the classic shoulder-hip-heel line while keeping the arms and lower back relaxed and following the forward movement of the stride. A brisk canter on grass will give the horse renewed enthusiasm during a schooling session. The rider will find it easiest to adopt a lighter seat position.

GALLOP

To ride a horse at this fast, exhilarating pace requires a secure seat and confidence in your ability to control the horse. The stirrup leathers should be shortened, so that the body lifts more easily out of the saddle, allowing the weight to come forward. The heels are well down, while the lower leg remains in the normal position. The rider should take care not to use the hands for balance in fast work.

▶ SCHOOL RULES ◀

Once you have progressed from your initial private lunge lessons into a school (arena) situation, you are likely to have to negotiate other horses and riders as well as control your own mount right from the start.

Apart from allowing other riders to get on with their work harmoniously and with respect for each other in the school or the warm-up area at competitions, the protocols used (the 'school rules'), as with driving on the road, are there to prevent collisions! They might initially seem hard to digest but once practised a little, the school rules become second nature, rather like the highway code.

Right: *Fine weather provides an opportunity for riders and horses to exercise in an outdoor school or open field.*

IN THE SCHOOL

Before entering the school, regardless of whether it is an outdoor school or an indoor arena, announce your presence loudly to warn other riders, who can then circle away from the door to give you clear access. 'Door please' or 'door clear' are commonly used announcements (in the USA, it is 'heads up'). Offer the same courtesy also when leaving the school, as

you can't assume everyone else is anticipating your next move. Riders can be very focused when they are concentrating on their work.

If you are entering the school already mounted, walk the horse onto the centre line or to the centre of a circle if you intend to stop and make any adjustments to the girth or stirrups. Similarly, if you are leading the horse, and intend to mount only once you are in the school,

Above and above right: *Riders do not always have the luxury of the school to themselves, so it is important to learn the school rules.*

move it well clear of the track before getting on. Horses in walk should always be kept off the main track and walked on the inner track, out of the way of others in trot and canter. When the school is busy, downward transitions to walk or halt are also normally performed on the inner track.

It is not only impolite, but also often unsafe to overtake another rider in the school. While working in a faster pace, if you have to pass another horse and rider, you should circle away and come back onto the track behind them, rather than pull out and cut in front of them. When working in a school formation, a safe distance of one horse's length should be maintained between each horse and rider at all times. During a lesson or schooling session, horses should be worked equally on both reins, so you have to get used to meeting other horses working on the opposite rein. If, for example, you are going to the right and the other rider to the left on the track, you should pass each other left hand to left hand. Therefore, if you are going to the right, it is up to you to move your horse onto the inner track for a safe distance to pass the other rider, then return to the main track, as the rider on the left rein has priority. The rider on the outside track also has priority over the rider on a circle, so the circling rider should come onto the inner track.

Inset: *Practising passing left hand to left hand as part of a group helps you to gain control of your horse.*

SCHOOL FIGURES

Classic school figures form the basis of dressage tests and also train beginners to ride accurately. The arena used for dressage training and competitions is marked out with a series of letters (called markers). There are two sizes of arena: 20 x 40m (22 x 44yd) for lower level tests and 20 x 60m (22 x 65yd) for any level up to grand prix. The letters A and C mark the entrance point and closed end of the arena respectively, with B and E denoting the half marks. The other letters in a 20 x 40m arena are M, F, K and H, located on the long sides, 6m (20ft) in from the short side. In addition there are two 'invisible' markers: D on the centre line midway between F and K, and G occupying the same position between M and H.

Above: *Schooling is a process of constant practice, until the basic exercises become second nature to both rider and horse.*

CHANGING THE REIN

- Riding terms can sometimes seem arcane, like 'Change the rein across the next diagonal', which simply means 'change direction' – in a school situation this makes more sense than: 'Change direction and go right or go left'. As a rider changes rein, he should, if in a rising trot, change diagonal by sitting for two beats of the trot at the point where the new direction is assumed, such as on reaching the track, or passing over X (see illustration on p139). To do this, both reins are taken into the whip-holding hand, while the free hand grasps the whip at the top and neatly pulls it through to the new position on the other side, taking care not to give the horse an inadvertent whack. When riding in a school, unless it is specifically needed on the outside, the whip is generally carried in the inside hand, to prevent it dragging on the walls of the school. While any change of direction counts as a change of rein, using the classic school figures ensures that the movement is beneficial to both riding technique and the horse's way of going.

- Changes of rein can be made either through two half-circles or one half-circle and return to the track, and are usually performed out of the corner at the end of a long side. The horse is ridden through a half-circle, then aimed at the track on a straight line with the new bend employed as the track is reached. A change of rein across the school, from E to B, for example, will be ridden as a quarter-circle, followed by a straight line, followed by another quarter-circle, before moving smoothly onto the track on the new rein.

SERPENTINES

- Serpentines help promote bend and looseness in the horse, and control, accuracy and 'feel' in the rider. The number of loops determines the difficulty of the exercise. Loops are ridden as a series of half-circles with straight sections in between. Serpentines can also be ridden as smooth bulb-shaped loops with changes of bend each time the horse crosses the centre line. With an even number of loops, the movement finishes on the same rein, whereas an odd number involves a change of rein.

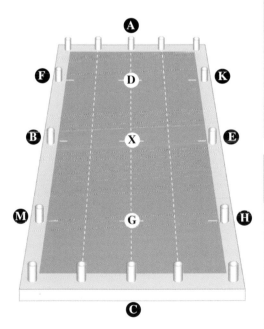

Above: *The arena used for dressage competitions is marked out with a series of letters (called markers) which denote where any given test movement is commenced or finished.*

CIRCLES

- The 20m (65ft) diameter circle is the preliminary circle for the novice rider to master while maintaining bend, balance and rhythm in the horse. The 20m (65ft) circle is made easy by the markers, as one half of the circle will be naturally described by the short side of the school. If your instructor calls: 'At A, twenty-metre circle', you will know that in a 20m x 40m (22 x 44yds) school, the circle will touch X. Similarly, a circle ridden in the centre of the school will touch the sides at E and B. Other schooling circles are 15m (50ft) and 10m (32ft). Smaller circles, known as voltes, are only performed by highly trained horses, as a greater degree of collection is needed to execute them correctly. A figure of eight, consisting of two circles with a change of rein, requires a change of bend through the centre of the figure.

LOOPS

- A simple exercise in change of bend, loops are ridden on the long side of the school, as a curve off the track. The return to the track is made at the midpoint (E or B) with a change of bend at each change of direction. A loop 5m (5.5yds) in from the track is furthest away from the track – 5m (5.5yds) – at the midpoint.

The first step towards expanding your horizons as a rider is to become competent at riding outside of the school environment. Riding in the open, or 'hacking out', is an important part of confidence-building and the education of both horse and rider.

While a young horse needs to be kept under control, and be sufficiently accepting of the rider to be safe enough to ride out, similarly the starter rider must establish security in the seat. The rider must demonstrate enough ability to control the horse within the school, before being able to ride out in safety. It is therefore important that less experienced riders are mounted on steady, familiar horses that are accustomed to hacking out, as horses used to being in the school tend to be somewhat 'on their toes' and forward-going when venturing into the great outdoors. Riding out unaccompanied is not something an inexperienced rider should attempt. When riding out in a group, more experienced riders should always be positioned at the front and back of the ride, and they should ensure that the duration, pace and the overall demands of the ride are tailored to the abilities of the least experienced rider in the group.

What form riding out takes is dependent on your area. Riders who live in the countryside have more opportunities for hacking out than those in towns and suburbs, but even so, most riders nowadays will have some housing areas and busy roads to negotiate, so it is important to be as aware of the highway code as the country code, and a great deal of attention must be paid to all aspects of safety.

Above: *Riding out is a sociable experience, but novices should always be accompanied by more experienced riders.*

Before hacking out, tack should be thoroughly checked for wear and tear. All riders must wear an approved, correctly fitted hard hat or crash cap. Not only is this a precaution for the rider, but in the event of any accident involving an insurance claim, it is important that essential safety precautions have been adhered to. Furthermore, riders who disregard the basic elements of safety are less likely to be afforded respect by nonriding road users and may well incur unpleasant comments from passing motorists.

If the first part of the ride is through a busy area, it is advisable to ride the horse in the school for a while to get it relaxed and listening. For the benefit of the less experienced or infrequent rider, this is also a chance to relax and get the feel of the horse.

As a general rule, horses should always be ridden in walk on surfaced (hard top) roads. On a familiar, safe part of the road, riders may trot for short, controlled, steady periods, but if a horse is ridden too fast on hard roads, it can cause concussion and damage to its legs. There is also the risk of slipping. One expects wet roads to be slippery, but oil build-up can mean that dry roads can be slippery too.

Vehicles, cyclists, pedestrians and other riders should always be passed in walk, and horses brought to a walk whenever traffic approaches. Not all road users are familiar with, or sympathetic towards, animals on public roads. Courtesy is vitally important, not only to thank the considerate driver who has given your ride a wide berth at a slow speed, but also to promote the reputation of riders as sensible road users.

A driver who has slowed to pass you is likely to be less helpful to the next group of riders he passes if all he's received previously is a glum expression and no acknowledgement. A hand raised in thanks, along with a smile, goes a long way towards keeping drivers on the side of riders.

In order to communicate changes of direction and pace, hand signals are used. The lead rider should indicate a turn via an outstretched arm to the right or left, which is then taken up by the rest of the ride. In a group ride, the front and back riders should be in charge of signals and an agreement made beforehand that this will not be the responsibility of the least experienced riders. A signal to the ride to slow down, or a request for traffic to slow down, is given by raising and lowering an out-

Inset: *Horses should only be ridden in walk or trot on hard roads, to prevent damage to their legs as well as to reduce the risk of slipping on wet or oily surfaces.*

stretched arm. If the ride is going to halt at a junction, for example, the lead rider will raise a hand and hold the position until all the horses have come to a stop.

Riders should move in single file on busy roads, but on quieter roads and riding tracks they can ride two abreast with a sensible span between each horse.

Cantering on an appropriate track, or around the edge of the field, should follow several periods of walking and trotting so the horses are warmed up and less fresh. When cantering on a group ride, it is safest to stick to the single file formation with the lead rider controlling the pace sensibly to safe-guard the less experi-enced riders.

If by chance any damage occurs on a ride, it is polite to report it as soon as possible. Farmers who allow riders to use the edges of their crop fields will soon put a stop to such favours if crops end up being tram-pled by out-of-con-

trol horses. Damage to gates or fences should be made good for the same reason and good relationships with farmers and land owners should be cultivated if riders are to be allowed the privilege of riding over their land. Needless to say, horses should not be taken on tracks or routes which specifically say 'no horses', even if a grassy track looks appealing. On foot paths

and public recreation areas, riders should be prepared, especially when in a fast pace, to slow down when approaching walkers, runners or cyclists. Avoid very wet, muddy tracks, not just because they can be dangerous for the horse's legs but because the impressions left in the mud by hooves will harden when the track dries out, leaving dangerous ruts.

The last part of a ride should be undertaken in walk to cool the horses before they return to the stables.

Riding out consists of not only being in control of the horse but also being aware of other situations that could affect one's enjoyment. The pace, duration and direc-tion of the ride should always be based on prevailing weather conditions, as well as the level of training and competence of the least-experienced horses and riders in the group.

To some novice riders, the number of things to think about on an outride may seem daunting, while to others it may be stating the obvious.

Riding in the open is supposed to be re-creational. It should be fun and a chance for less experienced riders to gain confidence in horses in a relaxed way, but even a Sunday afternoon drive through the country is only enjoyable if you are in control of your car and the situation on the road.

Inset: *Drivers who slow down to pass you should always be courteously acknowledged.*

Above: *Although some periods of an outride may be spent cantering or galloping, walking the horse back to the stables at the end of the ride allows it to cool down.*

OPENING AND CLOSING GATES

Gates should always be shut securely when the ride has passed through them, and this should be the responsibility of an experienced rider at the back of the group. Gate opening and closing takes a bit of practice for both rider and horse, but there is a specific way of accomplishing this task from horseback.

Approach the gate so the horse's body is more or less parallel to the gate, with its head towards the latch. With both reins and the whip in the outside hand, reach down and open the latch with the inside hand. When the latch is open, push the gate outward sufficiently for the horse to pass through without knocking itself, while keeping one hand on the gate so it does not swing away too far and you can retain control to close it. This will involve asking the horse to go forwards, then when its hindquarters are clear of the gap, stopping and turning the horse around its forelegs by using your inside leg behind the girth so the horse is back facing the gate as you push it to, and you are in position to close the gate with the new inside hand, having taken reins and whip into the new outside hand. Sounds complicated? With a bit of practice, and a horse that stands when asked, the manoeuvre becomes easier.

When a group has to pass through a gate, it is sensible for one rider to hold it open so the rest of the ride can pass. Never rely on gates staying open on their own, as a swinging gate can cause injury.

Above: *Learning to open and close gates without dismounting takes patience, and a horse that stands or moves when asked. With practice, however, it soon becomes a routine procedure.*

COPING WITH FALLS

Sooner or later every rider comes off their horse. In most cases, the only damage will be to your pride, but in order to avoid the worst, there are ways to cope with a fall that will help to minimize any real injury to you or your horse.

Perhaps the most important thing to bear in mind is that, in any situation where you are feeling nervous or uncertain, slow down, and where relevant, move to the side of the ride. Firstly, slowing down may help you to regain control and in the second instance, you are less likely to cause an accident or be ridden over by following riders if you are on the edges of a ride rather than in the centre of a fast-moving bunch. Falls occur in a variety of ways. You might lose your balance in the saddle and simply slide to the ground; or be thrown as the horse trips or stumbles. Whatever the type of fall though, try to land sideways and roll over your shoulder. If you are not hurt, get up as quickly as possible and remount. This is important, both for your own confidence and to re-establish control over the horse, particularly if you suspect that it has been instrumental in your fall.

If you have managed to keep hold of the reins, the horse should be standing still, waiting for you, but if you have let them go, your first task may be to catch it before you can remount. In the case of a horse that is now rel-

ishing its freedom, this can be quite a job. If a loose horse decides to make capture into a game, never chase it. With the help of other riders, try and corner it instead. Once it realizes that all its escape routes are blocked, it will give in. If a fall is as a result of a horse having stumbled or tripped, check its feet and legs carefully, perhaps even trot it up, before remounting, to ensure that the horse is still sound and able to continue.

Above: *If a fall can't be avoided, try to keep hold of the reins, and roll over your shoulder as you land.*

▶ RIDING WITH CARE IN THE COUNTRY ◀

Hacking in the open country forms the basis of the more formal discipline of cross-country riding and is an opportunity for the novice rider to develop his or her skills and confidence.

On country rides, novices must always be accompanied by more experienced riders, who should lead the way over jumps and other obstacles, showing the less experienced riders and horses how to do it. They will teach the novice to take a systematic and safe approach over a variety of natural obstacles, not just jump them haphazardly or without thought.

Once the rider has sufficient control to ride a horse outdoors with safety, it is time to start tackling different terrain. Learning to ride on hills or through wooded areas, and to negotiate ditches or water crossings is the next step to becoming a confident all-round horseman.

All new experiences should be practised at a walk before going on to trotting and cantering. Riding on slopes and undulating ground requires both a secure seat and the balance to adapt the rider's weight to the horse's centre of gravity. The light seat is adopted when riding

Top: *Riding on slopes or undulating ground requires a secure seat. Riders should always be prepared to dismount and walk if a hill seems too tough for the horse.*

is better to dismount and lead it, allowing it plenty of rein for easier movement.

In icy conditions, dismounting and leading the horse is often the safest choice. Try to avoid steep turns in these conditions, as it is easy for the horse to lose its footing and slip.

When riding through water, always take a known path with a firm, level base. If you are unsure of the best route, dismount and lead the horse through, or at least take a careful look before asking the horse to step into the water. On hot, sunny days riders should keep the horse moving forwards, to avoid any possible inclination for it to stop for a refreshing roll. Pawing the ground is a definite warning sign!

When riding in wooded areas, lean well forward when passing underneath overhanging branches. If you have used a hand to sweep aside a branch, do not allow it to whisk back onto the rider behind you. Either stop and hold the branch until the rest of the ride has passed, or release it slowly and allow the next rider to take hold of the branch and move it out of the way for themselves.

One of the pleasures of riding in the country is the opportunity to jump natural obstacles, such as logs, ditches and small stone walls. Riders should have had experience of jumping in the school before tackling outdoor obstacles and on no account should any natural fence or obstacle be attempted if it is bigger than the fences the horse (or rider) is used to jumping in the school. All natural obstacles should be inspected first to ensure that there are no sharp edges or unseen dangers on the other side.

When approaching a natural obstacle, such as a fallen tree across a bridle path, the rider should decide in advance whether to attempt it or go around the obstacle. Once a decision is made, the rider must ride on with confidence and approach the obstacle straight on and at a suitable pace.

uphill or downhill, with the rider's weight more out of the saddle when going uphill, to a degree that is dependent on the steepness of the incline.

Less experienced riders should use a neck strap when practising hill work, as it is very important that the horse has sufficient freedom of the head and neck to help maintain balance, and a rider hanging on for balance is counterproductive. The rider's heels should be kept down, while the knees and lower leg remain in secure contact with the horse's sides.

In deep, boggy ground, the rider should also use the lighter seat to take his or her weight more off the horse's back, and the horse should be given as much rein as necessary. If the horse is sinking into soft ground, it

▶ SAFE LONG-DISTANCE EXCURSIONS ◀

This covers anything from a full day's ride through countryside close to one's home, to week-long trails in different locations. Day or weekend rides are an opportunity to explore new areas on horseback, either by taking your own horse by horse box or trailer to stay with friends, or booking up for a day's ride in a new location. Long-distance trails can also be a fun way to enjoy the sights in a foreign country.

The key to undertaking both types of trails successfully is careful planning and a sound knowledge of your own riding ability and limitations, as well as the capabilities of the horse involved.

Before contemplating any long-distance riding, it is important for both the rider and horse to be fit. A tired rider sits more heavily on the horse's back, but frequent extended riding sessions, particularly in trot, will help to gradually build up the stamina required.

As riders must be prepared to dismount and walk alongside the horse, particularly on steep hills and long downhill stretches, comfortable boots and suitable clothes are a must.

All the tack and equipment used on long-distance rides needs special attention, as there is no quick recourse to the tack room for 'spares' should anything malfunction. In addition to the basic tack, the horse may also be asked to carry extra weight in the form of saddlebags containing the rider's gear, so much thought needs to be given to what to include.

On most recreational trails, all the gear and equipment is transported to the next overnight halt, but riders may need day-packs or saddlebags to take a warm sweater or jacket, snack foods and water, and basic first-aid items, including sunscreen in warm climates. You may also have to carry enough water and food for your horse.

Before taking your horse on any long-distance ride, especially if it is overnight, it is wise to have it checked by a veterinarian. The condition of the feet and shoes must be checked as well, and if required, new shoes fitted at least a week in advance of the ride.

Despite the fact that it may seem daunting, long-distance rides can be easily accomplished if they are broken up into sections of suitable lengths. If you plan your ride sensibly, you will be able to structure the pace and energy required so that both you and your horse are able to enjoy the activity and turn out each morning feeling fresh and ready for the next stage.

Inset: *Although bush hats are being worn as protection against the sun, novice riders should rather wear conventional hard hats or skull caps.*

▶ COMPETENT TRAIL RIDING ◀

Although there are many aspects to trail riding, such as competitive trails and endurance rides, most riders will focus on pleasure trail riding, which is a pleasant way of combining a vacation with riding. Trail riding has a great following in the USA, but is gaining in popularity worldwide, with the choice of countries and trails on offer increasing every year. As the name implies, pleasure trails are just that – a group of riders and horses making their way leisurely from one overnight stop to the next. These are the equine equivalent of hiking trails and most trail organizers go to great lengths to ensure that their trails pass through interesting and attractive countryside. Overnight stops may be in tented camps, farmhouses or log cabins, and riders can expect hot showers, cooked meals and a chance to relax with a cold drink at the end of the day.

Most trails supply horses, and riders wishing to take their own horses should enquire well in advance whether this is possible. Trail instructors will attempt to match horse and rider and it is up to you to be honest about the level of your riding skills.

Some trails offer different options for novice and experienced riders, so that groups with the same level of ability ride together. Other trails are taken at a slower pace throughout and are suitable for all levels of experience. In the USA, many trail operators offer the chance to ride in either western or conventional style, but this is worth investigating before you commit yourself to a holiday and arrive with your breeches and top boots to find your fellow riders in jeans and chaps. On most trails riders opt for casual gear, and those used to a more conventional approach should find out ahead of time what the normal practice is. American trails tend towards the 'cowboy' image, with many operators in states such as Arizona, Wyoming and Oregon.

In contrast, trail riders in Europe and the UK can take in the countryside, along with historic towns and villages, sleeping in castles, chateaux or country inns. In southern Africa and Australia, where the trails are through wilderness and open country, riders can get close to big game, or take part in a cattle drive on an outback ranch, often camping out overnight.

To get the most out of trail riding, it is preferable for riders to have achieved a minimum skill level, to be competent at all gaits, including the gallop, and to be confident of controlling an unknown horse in the open. Fitness and the ability to sit in the saddle for some hours at a time are important, and most trails have a maximum weight limit. As with any holiday, planning and booking ahead is essential for trail rides. Whether you want to improve your jumping, learn to round up cattle, or sightsee in another country, there is a trail somewhere in the world to suit your riding skills, needs and bank balance.

Inset: *Riders on a safari trail in the Okavango Delta have the opportunity to view big game animals from really close up.*

MAINTAINING GOOD HEALTH

The general attitude of any horse gives a good indication of his wellbeing. He should be alert and attentive all the time, and interested in things happening around him. His eyes should be bright and clear without any form of discharge, and the mucus membrane under the lids should be a salmon-pink colour rather than white, yellow or red. The insides of his nostrils, as well as the lips and gums, should also be salmon-pink.

If his head is hung low, chances are he is feeling poorly. His coat should shine, especially after he has been groomed. A dry coat, tight skin or evidence of sores, lumps and bald spots are reliable indications of poor health. Check his legs regularly, particularly after hard workouts and competitions. If they become puffy or swollen, or if you can feel heat, take immediate action. Unless you are certain of the cause and know what treatment is necessary, call the vet.

Check your horse's droppings daily. They should be green to golden-brown in colour, firm and moist, and should crumble when they hit the ground. Horses pass anything from eight to 15 piles a day. If there are very few, he may be

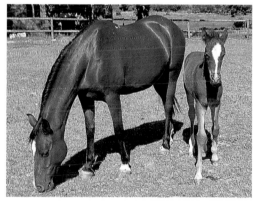

constipated; if there are none at all, something more serious may be wrong. If droppings are dry or slimy, smell offensive or contain blood, mucus or undigested food, you should be concerned. Dark urine is another sign the horse is not well. Inability to pass urine or straining when urinating could indicate an obstruction; excessive urinating is also abnormal. Loss of appetite and a refusal to drink water are sure indications that something is wrong.

Learn how to establish whether temperature, respiration, and pulse rate are normal, and be aware that these will definitely change during exercise and training.

Temperature is always a fair indication of health or sickness. Although you can use an ordinary thermometer, a veterinary thermometer is preferable. Lubricate the bulb end with petroleum jelly, lift the tail and insert it into the rectum. Remember to stand to the side of the hindquarters and, if you sense the horse may kick, get a helper to pick up one of the front legs. Hold the thermometer firmly, pressing it against the wall of the rectum for one or two minutes. Normal temperature is between 37.2°C and

Left: *A healthy horse is a happy horse. Take every precaution to keep it in peak condition.*
Inset: *Horses should have a shiny coat, and an overall indication of good health.*

38.3°C (99–101°F). If it is not within these limits, call your veterinarian.

Pulse rates of horses should be between 36 to 42 beats per minute when at rest. The easiest places to detect the pulse are at the artery just behind the elbow, under the jaw where there is a facial artery, or near the jugular vein in the neck. The most accurate way of taking the pulse is to use a stethoscope and the second hand of a watch to assess the number of beats per minute. Alternatively, count the pulse for ten seconds and multiply by six to calculate the pulse rate per minute. During exercise, the pulse or heart rate will increase dramatically. For instance, a horse walking actively will have a pulse rate of 60–70 beats a minute; after a short canter workout, it will rise to as much as 150 beats per minute. If the horse is at rest and his pulse is high, he may be in pain, have a fever, or simply be frightened.

Respiration rate refers to the number of breaths a horse takes every minute. When he is at rest, he should breathe in and out eight to 18 times – each in-and-out motion counting as one breath. To establish your horse's respiration rate, watch the rise and fall of the flanks or put your hand against his nostrils to feel the air on your hand. Like pulse rates, respiration rates increase during exercise and when a horse is ill or frightened.

▶ PREVENTING ILL HEALTH ◀

When it comes to the health of your horse, sensible preventative measures save not only heartache but also money in the long run. It stands to reason that horses that are not vaccinated against equine influenza (flu) and dewormed regularly are more likely to get sick than horses enjoying the benefit of this routine attention.

INTERNAL PARASITES

Internal parasites can cause major problems if neglected. In extreme cases, they can cause severe suffering and even death. Precautionary measures should be two-fold. The first step is to ensure that droppings are regularly picked up and removed from stables and paddocks. Fields and paddocks should also be rotated in order to ensure healthy grazing.

• Ensure that the horse is dewormed regularly to keep these harmful parasites to a minimum. There are various 'wormer' brands, which are available in either paste or powder format. To achieve maximum results, avoid using any one type or brand regularly. This will prevent worms from building up immunity. Whichever type you use, it is essential to give the correct amount. This is calculated by weight (see p83). Too little will be ineffective, while too much may lead to immunity and possibly even a sick horse. Make sure that you follow the manufacturer's instructions carefully and that you liaise with your vet for advice.

• Of several worms that infect horses, the worst is the large red worm (large

Above: *An intravenous injection administered by a qualified veterinarian.*

strongyle). This parasite lives in the gut or on the walls of the intestines and can cause considerable internal damage. Symptoms of infestation include loss of weight, a dull coat and diarrhoea.

- Small red worms (small strongyles) cause massive inflammation and ulceration of the horse's large intestinal wall, anaemia and constipation, and digestive problems.
- Roundworms are generally less of a problem, although they are often very long and infestation can be extensive. However, they can be a major problem in foals and young horses.

- Tapeworms sometimes occur and need to be treated, but are not common in horses.
- Bot eggs, laid by the troublesome gadfly (botfly), are tiny and difficult to remove. A special bot knife should be used to scrape the eggs off.

NOTE: External parasites can also be harmful, particularly ticks and lice. They are relatively easy to control with proprietary treatments, powders, shampoos and sprays, but can be a problem if neglected. Ask a vet for advice if you are unsure what to use or how often to treat for a particular parasite.

Vaccination requirements vary from country to country, so ensure you know which are required and when. Details will be recorded on a certificate or in the horse's passport to ensure they are carried out regularly, as required.

Some of the most common vaccinations include equine flu, tetanus and, in parts of Africa, African horse sickness. Most vaccinations are given annually, when the horse is not in work.

- **Tetanus** is a serious disease caused by bacteria in the soil that can infect wounds. It is often fatal. If a horse that has not been vaccinated against tetanus is wounded, call the veterinarian immediately – even a minor cut could lead to tetanus. Symptoms include stiffness and reluctance to move, overreaction to noise and loss of appetite. An initial course of injections, often combined with a flu vaccination, is followed by an annual booster.

- **Botulism** is a fatal toxin from feed contaminated by dead mice, rats, birds, and so on. Its effects are similar to tetanus.

- **Equine influenza** is a virus similar to the one that attacks humans. It is highly infectious and can be severe. In some countries, regular vaccinations against equine flu are mandatory, especially for competition and racehorses. Even if not compulsory, vaccination is advisable. There are different strains that can lead to breakdown in immunity. Although the vaccination cannot guarantee the horse will never get flu, symptoms will generally be milder. Like the tetanus vaccine, flu vaccines involve primary vaccinations followed by boosters. Your veterinarian will advise. (See also p179.)

- **Rhinopneumonitis** vaccinations are commonly given to horses in the United States and some parts of the United Kingdom. A contagious viral infection that causes colds in young horses, it also leads to abortion in

Top: *A nasal discharge could be serious. Check with your veterinarian to ascertain its cause.*

and in the United States horses travelling to competitions must be vaccinated against it annually. Initial symptoms include mild loss of appetite, low fever, depression and possible hypersensitivity to external stimuli. As the disease worsens, animals may appear blind or experience tremors, which may lead to paralysis. It is transmitted by insects, especially mosquitoes, and thought to be spread by wild birds. It is considered a significant public health issue as human infection can occur, usually resulting in brain damage or death. There are several strains, and vaccines are available for Western and Eastern equine encephalomyelitis.

- **African horse sickness** has been known to kill in epidemic proportions. A virus transmitted by midges, it is most common in hot, rainy conditions. Symptoms include high fever, swollen eyelids, heavy breathing and foaming at the nostrils. Animals can be protected by vaccination. During an outbreak, owners are advised to make frequent use of insect repellents and to stable their horses from late afternoon until mid-morning. Over the years there have been numerous embargoes on the movement of horses in parts of southern Africa as well as on the export of horses from that part of the world. There are various different strains of the disease and vaccinations are not 100 per cent effective.

pregnant mares. Young horses go off their feed, cough, have a nasal discharge and develop a fever. Unfortunately, pregnant mares may show no symptoms at all. Sick horses should be isolated and treated by a veterinarian, usually with antibiotics. The immune response of the vaccine is short-lived, so boosters are usually given quarterly.

- **Equine encephalomyelitis** is a serious viral disease for which there is no known treatment. It is restricted to the Americas,

Top: Swollen glands such as these are usually a sign that a horse is unwell and needs the attention of a vet.

Ponies and horses are also prone to numerous common ailments. While good stable management will keep these to a minimum, you should know what steps to take if they occur. When in doubt, call the vet.

nose. Coughs frequently accompany colds but may simply be due to an allergy. In the event of infection, take the horse off work and, if necessary, keep him in the stable. The vet will prescribe the required medication. (See also p178.)

COUGHS AND COLDS

An equine cold is similar to a human one, often starting with a rise in temperature and a runny

LAMENESS

This term refers to any horse or pony that is not 100 per cent sound. It may be due to an

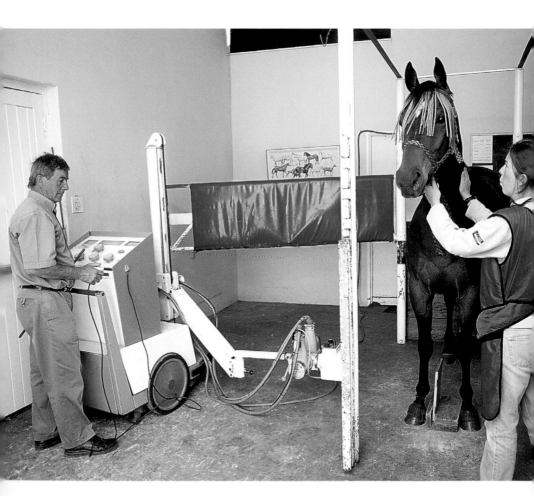

Above: *A horse has his leg X-rayed to ascertain whether or not there is evidence of injury.*

injured or strained tendon or a bruised sole after the animal has stepped on a stone. It may also be because the saddle does not fit correctly and the muscles in his back are sore. A horse may even go lame because he is not fit enough for the work he is being asked to do or because of incorrect shoeing.

It is usually obvious: the horse shifts his weight off the sore leg and may limp, appearing unbalanced. If you think your horse is lame, trot him out and ask your instructor or other experienced person to check his paces. Once you identify which limb is lame, feel for heat or swelling and check for wounds. If there is nothing obvious, an X-ray may be necessary. It is advisable to call a veterinarian to decide on treatment.

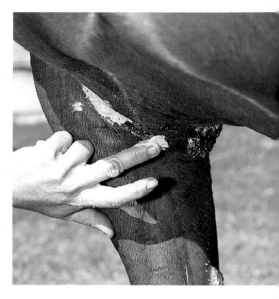

SADDLE AND BRIDLE SORES

These are usually caused by ill-fitting or dirty tack that rubs the coat and causes swelling or rawness. The girth can also rub away the hair and cause raw, bleeding sores. These conditions often occur because of ignorance and deteriorate because of neglect. Zinc cream may be used to heal the sores: persist twice a day until they dry out and heal. In severe cases, call the vet and rest the horse.

THRUSH

A bacterial infection that affects the frog of the horse's foot, thrush is often due to poor stable management, for example: wet, dirty stables; muddy paddocks; and feet that have not been properly cleaned or regularly attended to by the farrier. The foot of a horse with thrush smells and must be thoroughly cleaned, dried and treated with iodine, Stockholm tar or a suitable proprietary dressing.

SKIN CONDITIONS

- **Sweet itch** is an allergic condition caused by insect bites – probably a species of sandfly. The horse rubs himself against trees or paddock fencing to relieve the itch. It is most common along the mane and tail and results in ugly, inflamed patches. Use sweet itch lotion to relieve the sores, and fly repellent to keep the insects away.
- **Ringworm** is an infectious fungal condition not unlike human ringworm. It results in small raised patches that often become raw. Infected horses should be treated with proprietary lotions and their bedding burnt. Prevent its spread by using separate brushes and tack, and isolate a horse.
- **Contagious acne** looks a bit like ringworm, with small, round inflamed areas appearing on the coat, usually on the girth or saddle area. Like ringworm, it is infectious. It can be treated successfully with iodine-type products.

Top: *An antibacterial cream is applied to a deep wound to prevent infection.*

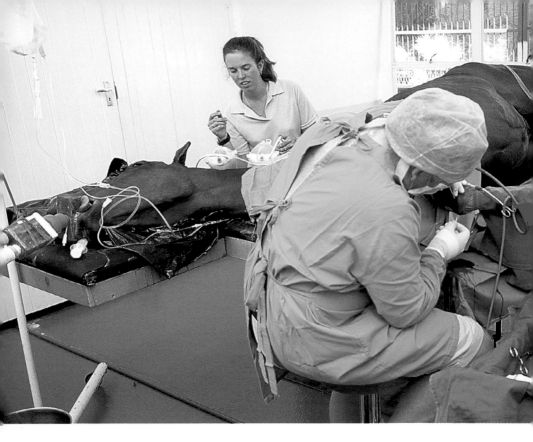

MUD FEVER (SCRATCHES)

Mud fever (scratches) and cracked heels are caused by a bacterial infection of the skin around heel and pastern. The infection tends to occur in wet, muddy areas, hence the name. The feet become sore and the legs swollen, with a yellow discharge from the skin. Using a barrier cream during exercise or when the horse is turned out can help. Avoid it by good cleaning, removing mud regularly and keeping the feet dry. Treatment involves the removal of scabs and swabbing with anti-bacterial wash, as well as trimming the heel feathers prevents accumulation of mud. When found over the back, the condition is known as rain scald (rainrot).

LAMINITIS

A very serious condition or syndrome, laminitis requires prompt treatment. Affecting ponies more often than horses, it is often caused by overfeeding. It results in inflammation and swelling of the feet, especially the front feet. Cold hosing of the feet will give temporary relief, but it is essential to call the vet. Badly conformed feet are more prone to the disease than those that are well conformed. A pony

Top: *When surgery is necessary, as with this horse having bone chips removed from its knee after an injury, the animal will need to be anaesthetized in a properly equipped veterinary surgery.*

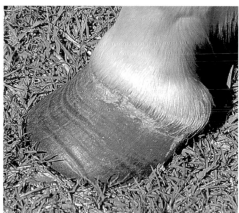

with laminitis should not be ridden until the condition has cleared. (See also p176.)

STRANGLES

A highly contagious disease aggravated by cold, wet weather, strangles is caused by the *Streptococcus equi* bacterium. Symptoms include a fever, loss of appetite, yellow nasal discharge and a moist cough. The horse may have difficulty in swallowing and the lymph glands swell dramatically. Isolate sick animals and call the vet. Strangles spreads rapidly and can be lethal in yards housing large numbers of horses.

BILIARY (PIROPLASMOSIS)

This is a contagious disease transmitted by ticks which affects the red blood cells in horses. Symptoms include loss of appetite, depression and fever. The mucus membranes become yellow and jaundiced, and the horse is often constipated. Biliary is a serious disease and can be fatal. If you suspect that a horse has contracted the disease, call the vet immediately.

Above right: *Abnormal rings around the hoof wall are the visible effects of severe laminitis.*
Top: *Mud fever (scratches) can be unsightly and painful.*

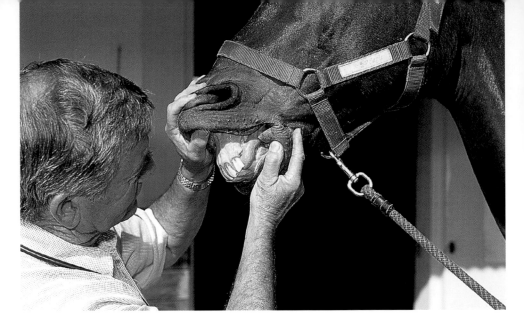

▶ TEETH ◀

Like humans, horses have two sets of teeth in a lifetime. By looking at the teeth you can estimate a horse's age, though you need a trained eye and an understanding of the structure of the teeth.

Most horses start losing their baby 'milk' teeth at about two-and-a-half years old. By the time they are four, they have most of their permanent teeth, though the canines usually only erupt when they are about five, at which point they have what is referred to as 'a full mouth'.

Unlike human teeth, the horse's teeth continue to grow throughout his life. Even though they are worn down when he chews and grinds his food, they need to be rasped or floated every six to 12 months with a long-handled rasp – a task done by a vet or equine dentist. The molars get very sharp edges over time and can cut the tongue and insides of the cheeks if this is not done.

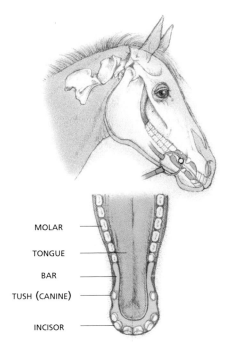

MOLAR

TONGUE

BAR

TUSH (CANINE)

INCISOR

Top: *A veterinarian checks for healthy gums and teeth.*

Equine dentists and some vets have more specialized tools that enable them to balance, float and rectify problems, including sharp hooks and waves, more effectively. The horse may need to be tranquilized, in which case a veterinarian will have to be present.

Horses and ponies also experience abnormalities of tooth eruption, so it is essential to check regularly that the mouth is developing naturally, particularly in young animals. If the eruption of the small underdeveloped teeth just in front of the upper molars, known as wolf teeth, coincides with a reluctance to accept the bit or uncharacteristic throwing of the horse's head, consider having them removed to relieve pressure and discomfort.

HOW TEETH AGE

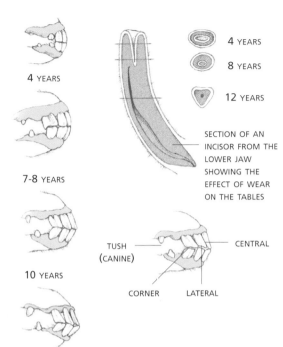

4 YEARS

7-8 YEARS

10 YEARS

15 YEARS

4 YEARS

8 YEARS

12 YEARS

SECTION OF AN INCISOR FROM THE LOWER JAW SHOWING THE EFFECT OF WEAR ON THE TABLES

TUSH (CANINE)

CENTRAL

CORNER   LATERAL

Above: *A veterinarian needs help to keep a horse's mouth open and the head still while he rasps the teeth.*

▶ OLD AGE ◀

Although not old, a horse over 10 years is referred to as 'aged' as it becomes more difficult to assess his age accurately from his teeth. However, horses generally live much longer.

As he ages, his physical condition may deteriorate. Once he is no longer ridden, muscle tone is reduced and the neck loses strength. Sunken hollows form around the eyes, the back becomes hollow and the withers appear more pronounced. Geriatric horses walk more slowly and carefully and may seem to be stiff.

A horse older than 15 years should be checked by the veterinarian at least once a year. Also check his teeth regularly as they are likely to break and eventually fall out. This will affect the way he chews and could impede digestion and lead to colic. As they age, horses lose their natural ability to regulate and maintain body temperature, so they should be properly rugged and given adequate protection in bad weather.

If you decide to retire your horse to a farm where he can live out his life in a well-grassed field, make sure regular veterinary attention is available and that there is sufficient shelter and grazing. Never abandon an old horse in a paddock: now, more than ever, he needs attention and companionship.

Above: *Old horses need a lot of attention, and companionship is all-important in the later stages of their lives.*

▶ THE IMPORTANCE OF EXERCISE AND FITNESS ◀

All horses need regular exercise to remain fit and healthy. Horses in the wild have plenty of room to gallop and get rid of accumulated energy. Stabled horses and those kept in restricted paddocks will need to be ridden and exercised regularly. If your horse is kept in a field, and there is sufficient space, he will have the opportunity to run around at will and may get plenty of exercise, but this does not mean he will necessarily be fit for work.

Hacking and schooling both contribute towards general fitness, but the programme you follow will depend on the time you have available, as well as the work you intend to do with your horse. For instance, if you are planning to event competitively, your horse needs to be considerably fitter than one required only for outrides at weekends. The dressage horse needs to be strong and muscular, so concentrate on achieving this. When you are getting a horse fit for jumping competitions, do not be tempted to jump excessively at home. Rather concentrate on steady flatwork, walking, trotting and cantering, and practising all the things you have learned in your riding lessons.

Remember that the more frequently you ride, the fitter you and your horse will become. However, unless you are preparing for endurance riding, this does not mean that you have to ride for long periods or even that you have to ride every day. Most instructors will assist in designing a fitness plan for your horse, which will include regular exercising, as well as riding and schooling. If your horse has been off owing to illness or injury, it is vital that you take great care to bring him back into work only very gradually.

Top: *Daily exercise is essential for maintaining your horse's health and fitness.*

If the horse is simply out of condition, it will take you six to eight weeks to get him back to reasonable fitness. A horse that has been off for three or four months will take at least the same period to get fit again. Remember your horse is an athlete and muscular strength will need to be built up slowly. Never rush a fitness programme: give the horse one day off a week.

1. Start by walking for 15 to 30 minutes, increasing gradually until you are walking for about an hour. This can take about three weeks – or even months if the horse has been resting because of a sprain or tendon injury. Horses become sound long before damaged tissue has been sufficiently repaired to withstand the stresses of normal work.

2. Introduce short periods of trot-work to begin building muscle tone. Combine this with periods of brisk walking, particularly up hills. Steady trotting on a hard road surface can be beneficial, but do not overdo this. Continue this way for about six weeks, increasing the trot-work to as long as two hours. In the case of a tendon or ligament injury, the trotting-walking phase should not start too soon and should continue for at least two to three months, but not for more than 30 minutes at a time. Eventually, introduce some slow cantering on the flat.

3. Now you can begin with serious schooling, and introduce some jumping if you wish. Increase the hill work and take him for a steady canter once or twice a week. Always start at a walk for about 15 minutes, then trot for a while before cantering. End with walking on a nice, loose rein.

Top: *A horse is worked out in the arena.*

Above: *Hacking is fun for horse and rider, keeping them both fit and healthy.*

EMERGENCIES

A healthy horse is a happy horse – a fact that usually helps any observant horse owner to identify illness or sudden injury. It should not take long to familiarize yourself with your horse's normal behaviour and demeanour, after which you should be able to identify any abnormal signs.

Of course, it helps to have a thorough knowledge of normal equine behaviour and a perception of what can go wrong. For instance, a healthy horse rolls for pleasure, whereas a horse with colic rolls in agony, and while all horses rest their hind legs when standing perfectly relaxed in the paddock or stable, it may indicate injury when a horse rests his front leg.

Take every possible precaution to keep your horse healthy — not only practising good stable management, but ensuring he receives routine veterinary treatments, including regular de-worming, teeth floating and all the necessary vaccinations to prevent illness.

Finally, you need to know what to do in an emergency and how to determine when it is necessary or advisable to call in a veterinary surgeon or other qualified practitioner.

All horse owners require the assistance of a veterinarian at some stage, even if the horse is perfectly healthy. Although all vets receive the same basic training, some specialize in horses, so even if your local vet normally looks after your dogs and cats, he or she may not be the best person to care for your pony or horse. Personal recommendation is a good way to find a suitable vet. Ideally, you want someone reasonably close to the stables; not only do most vets charge for travelling, but he or she will also be able to get to you more quickly in an emergency. Nonetheless, veterinarians do sometimes make visits to specific areas on certain days and, provided you use their services then, you will not be charged for transport.

Recently, a growing number of practitioners trained in fields such as physiotherapy, homeopathy, chiropractic and acupuncture have turned their skills to the care of horses. Others specialize in equine dentistry. In an emergency, always contact a veterinarian first. If you want to use other practitioners, you should ideally have your vet's support. If not, try to find one who will accept your desire to use alternative remedies.

Left: *If you know your horse, you will know when any behaviour seems out of character.*
Inset: *A well-equipped equine first-aid kit is an essential item in all stables.*

▶ VITAL SIGNS ◀

Having a record of your horse's normal pulse, respiration rate and temperature is extremely useful. To establish the average for your horse, readings need to be taken over several days, at the same time of day, while the horse is calm and at rest. Then, if there are any signs that the horse is off-colour, you have a point of reference for your veterinarian.

Typical respiration rate is between 8 and 12 breaths a minute at rest; pulse rate 36 to 42 beats per minute; and temperature 38°C (100.5°F). A healthy horse may sneeze on occasions during schooling, as this is a sign of concentration, but

coughing at the start of work is abnormal. See also Chapter 8, Maintaining Good Health.

TAKING THE HORSE'S TEMPERATURE

Although this can be done with an ordinary thermometer, a specialized equine one is preferable. Get someone to hold the horse, and if you fear it may kick, they can pick up a foreleg to prevent this. Shake the thermometer and lubricate the bulb with petroleum jelly. Stand beside the hindquarters, lift the tail and insert the bulb gently into the rectum. It is worth noting that the end you hold must be

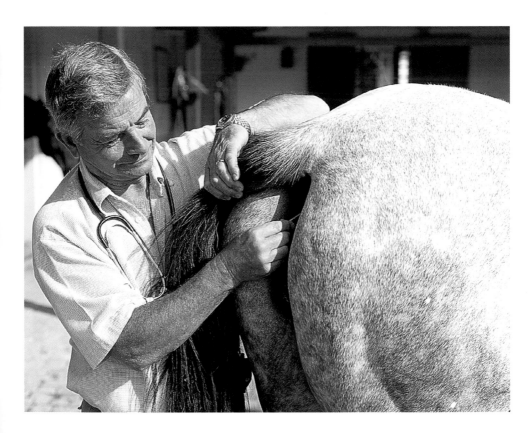

Above: *A vet takes a horse's temperature in the rectum using an equine thermometer.*

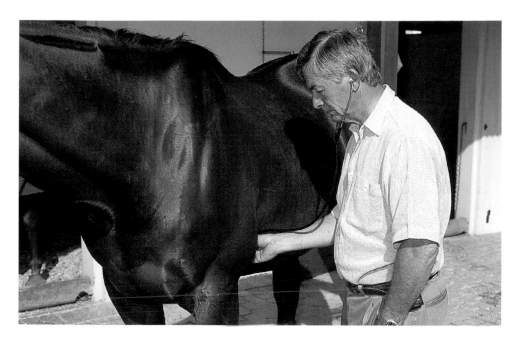

free of lubrication and you must hold it firmly. A horse's rectal muscles are very strong and it has been known for thermometers to disappear, necessitating a vet visit before you've even got this far. The thermometer should rest slightly to the side, or you may end up taking the temperature of a dung ball, and should rest in place for a minute before removal for the reading to be recorded.

TAKING THE HORSE'S PULSE

A stethoscope is the easiest means of recording this. Place the stethoscope just inside the horse's elbow to find a pulse and record, with the help of a watch with a second hand, the number of beats per minute. If you do not have a stethoscope, you can find the pulse in the same place with your fingers. Press lightly until you feel the pulse beating. There is also a big artery under the horse's jaw that can be used for taking the pulse, but it is harder to locate.

TAKING THE HORSE'S RESPIRATION RATE

Using a watch with a second hand, count the number of 'in' and 'out' breaths per minute by either observing the rise and fall of the flanks or feeling this by placing your palm below the horse's nostrils and feeling the air blowing over your hand.

MEASURING THE HORSE'S WEIGHT

To decide feed requirements and to gauge any change in weight, it is useful to record the horse's typical body weight using a proprietary weight tape (often obtainable from feed merchants). With the horse standing on a level surface, wrap the tape just behind the wither and to the back of where the girth normally goes. The weight can be read off the tape. Depending on its natural frame, a mature horse will weigh between 450 and 700kg (990 and 1540 lb).

Top: *A veterinarian uses a stethoscope to check the pulse of a horse. Between 36 and 42 beats per minute when at rest is normal.*

Having established any signs that the horse is off colour, further information that will be useful to your vet when you make the initial phone call is a résumé of your horse's work pattern and lifestyle. Is it stabled or turned out? Is it resting or in competitive work? What is the normal feed and, in the case of lameness, when was it last shod?

Generally speaking, the degree of pain the horse is displaying is a barometer as to how serious the condition is. However, severe colic indications (such as violent rolling and distress), acute lameness, choking, unwillingness to move or incapacity, breathing difficulties, injuries resulting in exposed bone, clear yellowish fluid (joint oil) leaking from joints, heavy bleeding, burns and eye injuries, can all be classed as emergencies.

Other conditions requiring veterinary attention include mild colic, diarrhoea, straining while defaecating, heat and swelling in limbs or feet, and laboured breathing. Cuts longer than 2cm (1in) need stitching, but puncture wounds and other wounds, especially near joints, will also need veterinary attention.

If you have called the vet out, ensure that you have the horse ready when he or she arrives. Vets are busy people and won't appreciate waiting around while you collect the horse from two fields away.

Tie the horse in a clean, well-lit area and remove all feed. In the case of wounds, ensure the wound is clean and undressed. If the feet are involved, have them already picked out. Have a bridle ready, as the horse may need extra restraint while the veterinarian examines a sore area. If the horse is lame, you will have to trot it up, so make sure an area is cleared for this, preferably on hard ground. In cases of suspected colic, it can be useful for the veterinarian to be provided with a fresh droppings sample.

Above: *The vet needs to examine the horse in good light and on a firm, clean surface.*

The priority when applying first aid to a horse, which may possibly be in a distressed condition, is safety. The horse should be restrained with a head collar (halter) or bridle and help employed from another pair of hands to hold it, as well as help to keep it calm by talking to and stroking it. When looking over a hindleg, hold the tail firmly down and to the side, or get your assistant to hold up a foreleg, to help prevent kicking. Grasping a fold of skin on the horse's neck can also act as an emergency restraint. Whatever has happened, it is vital that the handlers keep calm in order to keep the horse calm.

Be prepared for any emergency. Keep a first-aid kit at the stables and always take the essential items with you when travelling or competing. Check the expiry date of all medicines, and in the event of serious injury or illness, call the vet. Make sure you have:

- a selection of bandages, plus tape and pins
- gamgee (cotton encased in gauze)
- cotton wool and gauze
- a cold treatment pack

- salt (or saline water)
- antiseptic
- wound spray or cream
- antibiotic powder
- sharp scissors
- thermometer

- syringe
- Epsom salts
- leg poultices and cooling agents
- petroleum jelly

BLEEDING

Put on a bridle or head collar (headstall) and immobilize the horse, as movement will encourage bleeding. Ideally have someone else hold the horse. If blood is spurting from the wound, apply firm pressure with a cloth or dressing pad while the vet is called without delay.

If the blood is flowing more slowly, use a clean pad to apply pressure firmly to the area for about 10 seconds, then remove the pad. If the bleeding persists, reapply the pad and press firmly for longer. If the blood still flows after a few repetitions of this process, apply a clean pad to the wound and bandage it in place for half an hour. Remove and check. If the bleeding still has not stopped, apply a new pad and bandage for a further 30 minutes, but now is the time to call the vet if you have not already done so.

EYE INJURIES

Eye ointments should be gently laid in a line inside the lid, accessed by carefully pulling the lower lid down or upper lid up with a finger. Then close the eyelid. (This is often easier when someone else holds the horse.)

Above: *A bright, clear eye is a sign of health, but a dull or clouded eye could indicate a problem.*

WOUNDS

After flushing away any mud and debris, clean the wound and surrounding area with saline solution or a veterinary antiseptic diluted to the required strength (a syringe is useful for this). When the area is clean check the extent of the wound. Any wound over 2cm (1in) long will need stitching by the vet. Small cuts can be treated with wound cream or spray. If the cut is in a suitable place, cover it with a sterile dressing, add a layer of gamgee then hold the dressing in place with self-adhesive bandage secured with tape. Leg bandages can be finished with a stable bandage, but remember to bandage the other leg as well for support. Wise owners will make sure that their horse's tetanus vaccination programme is up to date.

Bumps, kicks, strains and sprains require treatment to reduce swelling. Hosing with cold water is the easiest method. When first applying the hose, direct it at the horse's foot and work it up the leg so the horse becomes accustomed to the idea. Continue to hose for about 15 minutes.

Alternatively, and in cases where there is no running water supply, apply a proprietary cold pack making sure it is not too cold, as it may cause a cold burn. Most cold packs consist of a gel that conforms to contours, so they can be bandaged into place. As a makeshift alternative, a packet of frozen peas is very effective.

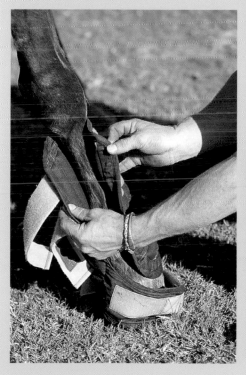

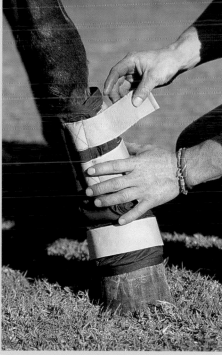

These warm, moist preparations draw dirt and infection from wounds and are often used for puncture wounds and for foot infections. They should never be used on a swelling without a wound and must be used with care near joints. Place the poultice, cut to the required size, on a plate and wet it with hot water for a few minutes. Drain the poultice (stacking another plate over the first and pressing firmly is a good way of doing this), and place a layer of plastic or cling film over the outside of the poultice. Position it over the required area, add a layer of gamgee and bandage

Above and above right: *While a poultice draws infection, a protective boot helps keep the foot dry and clean.*

ADMINISTERING MEDICINE

- Powders and liquid medicine can be added to feed. If necessary, disguise powder in a little molasses; this will also prevent the powder getting left in the manger.

- Pastes, such as wormers and other medicine, come in syringes with dose markers. Determine the required dose with your vet or, in the case of wormers, by the weight of the horse.

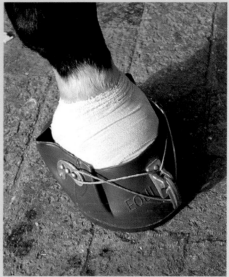

in place with a self-adhesive bandage. Foot poultices can be effectively held in place using a baby's disposable nappy (diaper). Applying wide adhesive tape over the bandage will preserve the base of the dressing as the horse walks on it. Alternatively, you could use a purpose-made protective boot which will protect the foot and keep it dry and clean.

Poultices should be changed two or three times a day as they are only effective while warm. They should not be used for more than a couple of days unless the veterinarian directs differently.

- Make sure the horse has nothing in its mouth. With one hand over the horse's nose, place the syringe in the corner of the mouth and squirt the dose with one efficient movement.

- Then hold the horse's head up to ensure that it swallows the lot. If you gently massage the underside of the jaw, you can encourage the swallowing movement.

Horse owners must be prepared to deal with a wide variety of ailments and emergencies. Readers are advised to take professional advice in all instances where a serious illness or injury is suspected. If in any doubt, call the vet first.

ACUTE AZOTURIA

This condition, also known as 'tying up', is caused by the build-up of lactic acid in the muscles, and causes weakness, pain, and in extreme cases, muscle damage. The horse becomes reluctant to move, the muscles over the back and loins become hard and painful, and the horse may strain to pass urine; if it does it will be very dark red in colour. If you are riding, dismount. Put anything handy (such as your jacket) over the horse's loin area to keep it warm and arrange to get the horse home in a horse box. Once in the stable, keep the horse warm with a rug.

ACUTE COLIC

Any abdominal pain is referred to as colic. There are types and degrees of colic, from spasmodic colic (spasms of the gut wall); to flatulent colic (caused by excess gas); to impaction or blockage in the large intestine. Colic can be caused by worm infestation, stress, or sudden alterations in diet. Treatment varies from the administration of antispasmodic drugs and painkillers, to liquid paraffin to dislodge blockages, to surgery. Colic surgery is very serious, but only some five per cent of colic cases require surgery. If you suspect your horse has colic, remove all feed and ensure the horse's bed is thick enough to prevent injury if it rolls. Walk the horse gently if it is standing. If it is lying down, do not allow it to roll; however, if it is rolling violently, keep out of the way to avoid injury to yourself.

ACUTE LAMINITIS (FOUNDER)

This occurs when reduced blood circulation in the foot causes the laminae holding the pedal bone to the front wall of the hoof to degenerate. Laminitis affects all four feet, but the front feet with more severity. In the initial stages the horse's movement will become restricted and 'pottery'; in extreme cases the pedal bone may start to rotate and drop. The condition can be caused by stress, and especially affects ponies on grass that is too lush. It is very painful. If the horse is in the field and able to walk, bring it into the stable. Remove all feed. If it is immobilized, just keep it calm until the veterinarian arrives. (See also p158.)

CAST HORSE

A horse is said to be 'cast' when it gets into such a position while lying in the stable that it is unable to get up on its own. If possible pull the front of the horse away from the wall. Once you have got the horse clear from the wall, move out of the way while it gets up. If it is still not able to get up on its own, you may need help, as rolling the horse over using ropes or lunge lines needs an accomplice.

Once it is on its feet, check the horse for any injuries and remake its bed.

CAUGHT IN BARBED WIRE

Get help, and get hold of wire cutters. This is a potentially dangerous situation as the horse is liable to panic, causing more injury to itself and possibly injuring those around it. If possible put a head collar (halter) on the horse to help hold it steady if it is standing. If the horse has fallen down, kneel on its neck and hold its head down to stop it struggling. Once the wire has been cut away, be careful to get out of the way when the horse gets up. Hose or wash the cuts and cover them with a clean, dry bandage or gauze pad. If stitches are required, keep the horse calm until the veterinarian arrives.

CHOKING

If a piece of apple or dry food gets stuck in the horse's throat, it may be dribbling and attempting to swallow with its head down and neck tensed. Horses cannot vomit but it is unlikely it will suffocate. Do not give the horse water, as fluid could go straight to the lungs. Call the vet, but while waiting you may be able to feel the obstruction and gentle massage may help to dislodge it.

FOOT PUNCTURES

If possible, remove the object but remember where on the foot it came from. A nail, for instance, might be easy to re-move, but any large or not clearly visible objects should be left in place until the vet arrives. Clean the area with water and, if possible, place the foot in a tub of warm water. Cover the area with a pad and bandage until veterinary advice can be sought.

FRACTURES

Broken bones occur most frequently in the horse's legs. A fracture may be indicated by sudden acute pain and swelling, often accompanied by the bone lying in an odd way. Keep the horse still until veterinary help arrives.

POISONING

Suspected poisoning may be revealed by symptoms similar to colic, along with diarrhoea, distressed breathing and sweating. If the horse is in the field, bring it into the stable. Remove all food and call the vet at once. Poisoning most often occurs from the ingestion of poisonous plants. If your paddock management is done properly, such plants will have been removed.

SEVERE TENDON INJURIES

Severe strain can cause the tendon fibres to tear or snap, which will drop the fetlock low to the ground. Keep the horse as still as possible, restrict its mobility and seek veterinary attention. In the meantime, hose the horse's leg with cold water to reduce pain and swelling, and apply a cold pad and bandage for support.

ABSCESS

Build-up of infection under the skin causing a painful lump. Treat with hot compresses to encourage drainage. Long-standing abscesses may be lanced by the veterinarian. When this happens or an abscess bursts, protect the surrounding skin by applying a barrier cream. Wash the area with saline solution to flush out any remaining infection, then apply antibiotic cream or the veterinarian's prescription.

ANAEMIA

If the horse is dull, listless and lethargic and the mucous membranes around the eyes and mouth look pale, a blood test may establish anaemia.

ARTHRITIS

The inflammation of joints caused by wear and tear, predominantly found in older horses. Often manageable under veterinary direction, it can also be treated with herbs and alternative remedies.

ARTHROSIS

Common in older horses, this is a condition which results in abnormal bone growth on the edges of joints, such as ringbone on the pedal, pastern or fetlock joint, and spavin on the lower hock joint. Specialist veterinary treatment

helps, as does special shoeing, but the condition will result in varying degrees of lameness.

CAPPED HOCKS

Swellings around the point of hock caused by abrasion. Capped hocks are usually prevented by the provision of good bedding.

CHRONIC OBSTRUCTIVE PULMONARY DISEASE (COPD)

This occurs when the horse's airways become obstructed by thick mucus and breathing is impaired. It is caused by a reaction or allergy to the fungal spores found in hay and straw. The horse will need to be managed in as dust-free an environment as possible on a permanent basis. Veterinary treatment may include antihistamines and/or the use of bronchodilators to clear the airways.

CORNS

Pressure sores or bruises on the sole of the foot causing pain and lameness. Often caused by ill-fitting shoes or waiting too long to replace shoes. They are difficult to spot. On removing the shoe, the vet will cut away the affected horn. Poulticing can draw out latent infection and the horse may require special pressure-relieving shoes.

COUGH

Can be a symptom of an allergy or virus and thus will be accompanied by other symptoms. Will need expert diagnosis to find the cause. (See also p156.)

CRACKED HEELS

Occur in wet and muddy conditions, when the back of the pastern becomes cracked and inflamed with thickening of the skin. It can be prevented by ensuring the heels are kept as dry as possible in such conditions. Treat with applications of antibacterial ointment.

DEGENERATIVE JOINT DISEASE (DJD)

Arthritis caused by stress on the joints.

DEHYDRATION

Particularly in hot weather or during intense competition, the horse may need additional electrolytes to replace lost fluids, salts and minerals. An indication of dehydration is if the skin does not return flexibly when it is pinched. In extreme cases, dehydration can contribute to azoturia or 'tying up'.

EPIDEMIC INFLUENZA VIRUS

Symptoms include a high temperature, nasal discharge, cough and swollen glands under the jaw. It is highly infectious, but can be prevented by vaccination. (See Vaccination, p154.)

FUNGAL INFECTIONS

Fungal infections, visible as bald, crusty patches on the skin, tend to spread through yards. In the case of an outbreak, all tack and equipment must be treated to prevent re-infection. Horses with fungal conditions should not travel. Treat with antibiotics or antifungal wash.

GALLS

Swollen, sensitive patches on the skin caused by ill-fitting tack, so the cause needs to be identified and removed. Once galls have healed, hair loss may be replaced by white hairs.

LICE

Small skin parasites which irritate the skin, causing raw patches. Common in under-conditioned animals. As well as treating the horse with antilice shampoo, all tack and equipment needs to be treated to prevent re-infection.

LYMPHANGITIS

An inflammation of the lymphatic vessels. Known as 'Monday morning disease' as it commonly occurs when animals are left in the stable on full feed rations, and not exercised. Recognizable by swollen, puffy legs and treated by gentle walking to improve circulation, cold hosing to reduce swelling, and reduction of feed the night before and during rest days as a preventative measure.

NAVICULAR DISEASE

A chronic condition, which appears as gradual lameness in one or both front feet. Corrective shoeing and prescription drugs to stimulate circulation can alleviate the condition.

NETTLE RASH / URTICARIA (HIVES)

This occurs as patches of raised swellings which tend to suddenly appear, then disappear just as quickly. It can occur in connection with other illnesses, or as an allergy to drugs, a particular feed or nettles. Usually harmless, but if it becomes excessively irritating the vet can prescribe a painkiller.

OVERREACH

A bruise or wound caused by the hind foot striking the heel of a front foot. This can be prevented by the use of overreach boots during exercise, especially fast work and jumping. Treat by cleaning the area thoroughly, use a poultice for a short period if the area is very dirty, and apply antibiotic dressing. The vet should be called if the wound is large or deep, or if the swelling is excessive, as this may be an indication of deeper damage.

PERIODIC OPTHALMIA

Also known as 'moon blindness'. This is a disease of the eye, which can occur suddenly and tends to recur. Little is known about the disease, which causes the cornea to become white and milky, the pupil to constrict and the eye area to become inflamed. It can eventually lead to blindness in the affected eye, but though there is no definitive treatment, prompt veterinary action can prevent permanent damage.

PUS-IN-THE-FOOT

This is a common condition arising usually from a puncture to the sole of the foot, which causes inflammation within the foot. The horse will be acutely lame and the foot will feel hot. The veterinarian will cut away the horn in the area of the abscess to drain the infection. A poultice must be applied two or three times a day until all infection is drawn out, and the foot must be kept bandaged. The hole can then be plugged with cotton wool soaked in antibiotic spray. The application of a sugar and iodine paste over the area will help to harden the horn.

QUITTOR

An infection located at the coronary band (the cartilage on the side of the foot). It is caused by injury or a puncture, and is signified by swelling, inflammation and pain. The veterinarian will treat it with antibiotics.

SANDCRACK

A vertical crack in the hoof caused by injury or poorly cared for feet. Cracks require special care from the farrier, who may insert clips or fill the crack with synthetic paste until it has grown out.

SARCOIDS

Horny, tumour-like warts on the surface of the skin which, if they get very large, may rub or become infected. In this case they should be removed surgically. Sarcoid warts can recur.

SEEDY TOE (SEPARATIONS)

When the hoof wall separates from the sole at the toe. If the sensitive tissue becomes inflamed, lameness will ensue. The farrier or veterinarian will cut away dead horn and dress the foot.

SPLINTS (PERIOSTITIS)

Bony formations which arise between the splint bone and cannon bone, usually in growing horses, or through stress.

While forming, they can cause short-term lameness. Cold packs can alleviate any inflammation. A vet may administer cortisone injections.

TETANUS

Every horse should be regularly vaccinated against this infection of the nervous system, which is caused by bacteria entering a wound. At the first signs of tetanus seek advice from a vet erinarian immediately. (See Vaccination, p154.)

WINDGALLS

These are painless, soft swellings usually found at the back of the leg, just above the fetlock joint. They are unsightly but harmless. Stable bandages and support bandages while exercising can help prevent the tendency to windgalls. A soft swelling located just above the hock joint is known as a thoroughpin.

WORMS

There are various forms of infestation to which a horse may be susceptible, depending on the season, the age of the horse and, to some extent, the area. Prevention measures include good paddock management and regular dosing with antiparasite drugs. Worm infestation can be serious, even fatal in some cases, so control is essential. (See Internal Parasites, p152–53)

Alfalfa: Green fodder also known as lucerne.

Bell boots: Bell-shaped boots (or overreach boots) to protect a horse's hooves.

Blanket: Spotted pattern found on some Appaloosa horses.

Bot: Parasite that infests horses.

Breastplate: Strap designed to prevent saddles from slipping backwards.

Breed: A specific equine group which has been bred selectively to achieve a clearly defined set of characteristics.

Bridle: Headgear incorporating bit and reins, used to control horses.

Brushing boots: Boots used to protect the base of the leg; also called splint boots.

Cannon bone: The bone between the hock and fetlock.

Cantle: Back point of a saddle.

Cavesson: Standard type of noseband.

Clinch: Part of a horseshoe nail that is bent over to secure the shoe.

Conformation: The way a horse is formed, with particular regard to its proportions.

Coolers: Sweat rugs and sheets used after exercise or under thicker blankets to prevent the horse getting chills.

Coronet: Area above the hoof at the base of the pastern.

Crest: Top line of the neck.

Croup: Hindquarters or rump.

Curb: Chain used with curb bit that fits under a horse's chin.

Currycomb: Used to rub down a horse's coat; metal version used only to clean body brushes.

Dandy-brush: Hard brush with long, stiff brushes, used to brush the coat but not the tail or mane.

Dock: Thick fleshy part at top of the tail.

Double bridle: Bridle with two bits (curb and bridoon) and two sets of reins.

Draught horse: Horses used for pulling carts and carriages.

Dressage: Training a horse to perform manoeuvres in response to the rider's signals. It developed into an elegant equestrian art and sport.

Eel stripe: Continuous dorsal stripe of black, brown or dun hair from neck to tail; most common in dun-coloured horses.

Endurance: Marathon event on horseback.

Ergot: Horny growth on back of fetlock joint.

Eventing: Competitive discipline to test horsemanship; combines dressage, show jumping and cross country.

Fetlock: Ankle or joint behind pastern-joint; often with feathers.

Flash noseband: Strap attached to front of cavesson noseband and fastened under chin.

Flehman: Action a horse makes by curling its lips and lifting its heads when smelling the air.

Float: Action of equine dentist or veterinarian when rasping the teeth.

Fly sheets: Summer or day sheets used to protect horses that could develop bleaching or pigmentations in the sun.

Forelock: Mane hair that hangs over the forehead, between the ears.

Frog: Rubbery pad of horn in the sole of the foot that acts as a shock absorber.

Fulmer: Bit with cheek bars on either side; useful for horses with a tendency to nap or run out at jumps.

Gag: Type of bit; more severe because of its poll action.

Gait: The movement of a horse; walk, trot, canter, gallop.

Gamgee: Cotton or cotton wool encased in gauze.

Girth: Circumference of a horse's body around its middle; also the strap that extends around the stomach (or girth) to keep the saddle on.

Grakle: Type of noseband, with straps crossing over the front of the nose; favoured by cross-country riders.

Hack: Ordinary pleasure riding; also a specific type of light riding horse.

Halter: Head collar used with a lead-rein or rope to lead or tie up a horse.

Hand: Term of measurement to describe horses' height; one hand (hh) equals 10.16cm (4in).

Harness: Equipment for driving horses.

Hay net: Net designed to hold hay, straw, etc, so that it may be tied up off the ground.

Hocks: Joints between knee and fetlock.

Hogged mane: Mane from which all hair has been removed by clipping; also known as a roached mane in America.

Kineton noseband: Design that prevents free movement of the horse's jaw; used to school horses and ponies that pull.

Leopard: Blanket with egg shaped spots on white Appaloosa horses.

Lucerne: Plant used for fodder; known as alfalfa in some parts of the world.

Lunge: Circular exercise/training of horses.

Marble: Mottled pattern found on some Appaloosa horses.

Martingale: Straps used to gain extra control of the horse and stop him from raising and throwing his head; various types including standing and running.

Muck out: Removal of droppings and cleaning out stables.

Muzzle: Area around nostrils and mouth.

Numnah: Saddle pad or saddlecloth used under the saddle.

Pastern: A part of the horse's foot between the fetlock and hoof.

Pelham: Type of bit that combines a curb and bridoon or snaffle on one mouthpiece.

Piebald: The term used (especially in the United Kingdom) to describe colouring of a pony with black and white patches on its body.

Points: Muzzle, mane, tail, leg extremities and tips of ears.

Poll: Top of a horse's head.

Pommel: The projecting front part of a saddle.

Quarters: Hindquarters or rump.

Saddle pad: See numnah.

Show jumping: Competitive jumping on horseback.

Skewbald: Term used (especially in Britain) to describe colouring of a pony with coloured and white (not black) patches on its body.

Snaffle: Mildest bit type; snaffle bridle incorporates a snaffle bit.

Snowflake: Pattern of white spots concentrated on the hips of some Appaloosa horses.

Stifle: Joint between hip and hock.

Stirrup: Foot rest for rider; attached to stirrup leather attached to saddle.

Stock horse: Horse used for rounding-up sheep or cattle

Stud: Breeding establishment; also refers to metal elements manufactured for use in horseshoes to help prevent slipping.

Surcingle: Girth-like strap/overgirth that fits over the saddle and girth; used during eventing; blanket surcingle is used to secure rugs.

Tack: Abbreviation of 'tackle'; all saddlery including bridle and saddle.

Tendon boots: Open-fronted boots similar to brushing boots, but designed to protect tendons and fetlocks.

Thrush: A bacterial infection affecting the cleft of the frog of the foot.

Turnout: General appearance of horse and rider in relation to dress, cleanliness of tack and thorough grooming.

Wall: Visible part of the hoof.

Walleye: White or blue-white eye due to a lack of pigment; also called 'glass eye'.

Wind sucking: A potentially harmful stable vice where the horse sucks in air.

Withers: Ridge between the shoulder-blades.

▶ INDEX ◀

Note: Page numbers in **bold** refer to all illustrated material.

▶ FEI NATIONAL FEDERATIONS ◀

Fédération Equestre Internationale (FEI)
PO Box 157, 1000 Lausanne 5 Switzerland
Tel: + 41 21˙310-4747
Fax: + 41 21 310-4760
http://www.horsesport.org
has 128 member countries, including:

Australia
Equestrian Federation of Australia
Level 2, 196 Greenhill Rd, Eastwood
SA 5063
Tel: + 61 88 357-0077
Fax: + 61 88 357-0091
email: info@efanational.com

Austria
Bundesfachverband für Reiten und Fahren
in Österreich
Geiselbergstrasse 26-32/512, Wien 1110
Tel: + 43 1 749-9261
Fax: + 43 1 749-9291
email: office@fena.at

Belgium
Fédération Royale Belge des Sports Equestres
Avenue Houba de Strooper 156
Bruxelles 1020
Tel: + 32 2 478-5056
Fax: + 32 2 478-1126
email: info@equibel.be

Canada
Equine Canada
2460 Lancaster Road, Suite 200
Ottawa, Ontario KIB 455
Tel: + 1 613 248-3433
Fax: + 1 613 248-3484
email: dadams@equestrian.ca

France
Fédération Française d'Equitation
Immeuble le Quintet, Bâtiment E 81/83 Avenue
E. Valliant, Boulogna, Billancourt 92517 Cedex
Tel: + 33 1 5817-5817
Fax: + 33 1 5817-5853
email: dtnadj@ffe.com

Germany
Deutsche Reiterliche Vereinigung
PO Box 110265, Warendorf 48231
Tel: + 49 2581 6-3620
Fax: + 49 2581 6-2144
email: fn@fn-dokr.de

Ireland
Equestrian Federation of Ireland
Ashton House
Castleknock, Dublin 1515
Tel: + 353 1 868-8222
Fax: + 353 1 882-3782
email: efi@horsesport.ie

Italy
Italian Equestrian Federation
Viale Tiziano 74-76, 00196 Rome
Tel: + 39 6 3685-8105
Fax: + 39 6 323-3772
email: fise@fise.it

Netherlands
Stichting Nederlandse Hippische Sportbond
PO Box 3040, Ca Ermelo 3850

Tel: + 31 577 40-8200
Fax: + 31 577 40-1725
email: info@nhs.nl

New Zealand

New Zealand Equestrian Federation
PO Box 6146, Te Aro, Wellington 6035
Tel: + 64 4 801-6449
Fax: + 64 4 801-7701
email: nzef@nzequestrian.org.nz

Norway

Norges Rytterforbund
Serviceboks 1u.s.
Sognsveien 75, Oslo 0840
Tel: + 47 21 02-9650
Fax. + 47 21 02-9651
email: nryf@rytter.no

Portugal

Federaçao Equestre Portuguesa
Avenida Manuel da Maia No. 26
4eme Droite, Lisbon 1000-201
Tel: + 351 21 847 8774
Fax: + 351 21 847-4582
email: secgeral@fep.pt

South Africa

SA National Equestrian Federation
PO Box 30875, Kyalami, 1684 Gauteng
Tel: + 27 11 468-3236
Fax: + 27 11 468-3238
email: sanef@iafrica.com

Spain

Real Federaçion Hipica Espanola
C/Ayala No. 6, 6o drcha, Madrid 28001

Tel: + 34 91 436-4200
Fax: + 34 91 575-0770
email: rfhe@rfhe.com

Sweden

Svenska Ridsportförbundet
Ridsportens Hus, Strömsholm
Kolback 73040
Tel: + 46 220 4-5600
Fax: + 46 220 4-5670
email: kansliet@ridsport.se

Switzerland

Fédération Suisse des Sports
Equestres
H Case Postale 726
3000 Berne 22
Tel: + 41 31 335-4343
Fax: + 41 31 335-4357/8
email: vst@svps-fsse.ch

United Kingdom

British Equestrian Federation
National Agricultural Centre
Stoneleigh Park, Kenilworth
Warwickshire, Warcs CV8 2RH
Tel: + 44 24 7669-8871
Fax: + 44 24 7669-6484
email: info@bef.co.uk

United States of America

USA Equestrian Inc.
4047 Iron Works Parkway
Lexington 40511-8483KY
Tel: + 1 859 258-2472
Fax: + 1 859 253-1968
email: sfrank@equestrian.org

Baird, Eric. (1977). *Horse Care*. London: Macdonald and Jane's.

Belton, Christina (translator). (1997). *The Principles of Riding: The Official Instruction Handbook of the German National Equestrian Federation* – Part 1. Addington, Great Britain: Kenilworth Press.

Bird, Catherine. (2002). *A Healthy Horse the Natural Way*. Sydney: New Holland Publishers.

Callery, Emma (ed). (1994). *The New Rider's Companion*. London: The Apple Press.

Cooper, Barbara. (2000). *The Manual of Horsemanship*. London: The Pony Club.

Culshaw, Doris. (1995). *Bits, Bridles & Saddles*. London: B. T. Batsford.

Draper, Judith. (1999). *Illustrated Encyclopaedia: Horse Breeds of the World*. London: Sebastian Kelly.

Edwards, Elwyn Hartley (ed). (1977). *Encyclopaedia of the Horse*. London: Octopus Books.

Edwards, Elwyn Hartley. (2000). *The New Encyclopaedia of the Horse*. London: Dorling Kindersley.

Faurie, Bernadette. (2000). *The Horse Riding & Care Handbook*. London: New Holland Publishers.

Fitchet, Peter. (1991). *Horse Health Care*. Johannesburg: Delta Books.

Green, Carol. (1990). *Tack Explained*. London: Ward Lock.

Hawcroft, Tim. (1983). *The Complete Book of Horse Care*. Sydney: Weldon Publishing.

Iwanowski, George. (1987). *You and Your Horse*. Pietermaritzburg: Shuter & Shooter.

Janson, Mike and Kemball-Williams, Juliana. (1996). *The Complete Book of Horse & Pony Care*. Avonmouth, Great Britain: Parragon.

Kidd, Jane. (1981). *An Illustrated Guide to Horse and Pony Care*. London: Salamander Books.

Knox-Thompson, Elaine and Dickens, Suzanne. (1998). *Pony Club Manual No. 1 & No. 2*. Auckland: Ray Richards Publishers.

McBane, Susan. (1992). *Ponywise*. Addington, Great Britain: Kenilworth Press.

McBane, Susan (ed). (1988). *The Horse and the Bit*. Ramsbury: The Crowood Press.

Pilliner, Sarah (1994). *Prepare to Win: Care of the Competition Horse*. London: B.T. Batsford.

Powell, David G. and Jackson, Stephen G. (1992). Harlow, England: Longman Scientific & Technical.

Swift, Penny and Szymanowski, Janek. (2001). *The Sporting Horse in Southern Africa*. Cape Town: BoE Private Bank.

Web Sites

www.all-about-horses.com (links to numerous sites about horse care, riding, etc)

www.aro.co.za (global racing results and racing industry information; more than 500 000 Thoroughbred pedigrees)

www.equineinfo.com (magazine-type site with lots of links)

www.horsecity.com (varied site that includes news, health information, tips and games)

www.horsedaily.com (international news for people with a passion for horses)

www.horsefun.com (links to several international Pony Clubs; games, pictures and stories for children)

www.horsejunction.co.za (comprehensive site with loads of relevant information)

www.montyroberts.com (home site of the world's most famous 'horse whisperer')

www.sportinghorse.co.za (focus on sporting horse activies; also stallion register, articles, photographic library)

www.thehorse.com (guide to equine health care)

www.worldofhorses.co.uk (news and information to keep your horse healthy)

▸ PHOTOGRAPHIC CREDITS ◂